The

# 5-Minute
# BIBLE
# STUDY

for a

# Less Stressed
# Life

Print ISBN 978-1-63609-147-1

Published by Barbour Publishing, Inc., 1810 Barbour Drive, Uhrichsville, Ohio 44683, www.barbourbooks.com

*Our mission is to inspire the world with the life-changing message of the Bible.*

Member of the
Evangelical Christian
Publishers Association

Printed in the United States of America.

# The
# 5-Minute
# BIBLE STUDY
## for a
# Less Stressed Life

CAREY SCOTT

BARBOUR
PUBLISHING

# INTRODUCTION

How can you live a less stressed life when it feels like stress is a constant companion? The truth is, there is much to worry about between family, friends, career, health, finances, and a million other things. In your desire to live and love well, too often you end up full of anxious thoughts and overwhelming fears. But this isn't God's plan for your life. His hope is that you invite Him into the unsettling moments so His peace can bring comfort. And in His Word, you will find strength to grab hold of your faith and wisdom to release the stress tangling you up.

Let this book guide you on your journey to peace. It makes it easy and quick to discover what God says about stress-free living every day—even if you only have five minutes!

Minutes 1 – 2: **Read** the scripture passage for each day's Bible study.

Minute 3: **Understand.** Chew on a couple of thought-provoking statements that will challenge you and offer perspective in your own life.

Minute 4: **Apply.** Read a brief devotional that will help unpack the scripture passage and how it applies to your life today.

Minute 5: **Pray.** Use the sample prayer as is, or let it be a prompt as you talk to God. Don't forget to listen. He has things to say to you too.

*The 5-Minute Bible Study for a Less Stressed Life* is the perfect way to help you make time to dig into the Bible. His Word is alive and active, and relevant to your life right now. And even though you're busy, finding five minutes of guided God time is doable! Even more, it will make a noticeable difference in your pursuit of less stress and more peace!

# PULLED IN DIFFERENT DIRECTIONS

—————— Read Philippians 4:4–20 ——————

## Key Verse:

*Don't be pulled in different directions or worried about a thing. Be saturated in prayer throughout each day, offering your faith-filled requests before God with overflowing gratitude. Tell him every detail of your life, then God's wonderful peace that transcends human understanding, will guard your heart and mind through Jesus Christ.*

PHILIPPIANS 4:6–7 TPT

## Understand:

- Think about all the obligations and responsibilities pulling you in different directions right now. When you are stressed out, how do you respond? Quick to tears? Short-tempered? Emotionally shut-down? Paralyzed with fear? How do your common responses need to change based on today's reading?

- Can you remember a time when you felt God's peace? How does that compare to what you're feeling right now?

*Apply:*

There is no doubt this life pulls us in a million different directions. Between family responsibilities, career
expectations, personal care, and other worthy obligations, we can easily find ourselves frazzled and stressed
out. But it doesn't have to be this way. Anxiety doesn't
have to be our automatic response to a busy schedule.

What if every time you started feeling stress rise
up, you prayed? So when you're running late for car-
pool, you ask for a sense of calm. When the deadline
gets moved up, you ask God for laser focus at work.
When you're struggling to fit in a workout, you ask the
Lord for better time management. Talk to your Father.

Remember we serve a God of order, not chaos.
And when we need it the very most, He will bring us
into a place of peace. Be quick to ask for His help.

*Pray:*

*God, thank You for being willing to help me when
life feels overwhelming. Sometimes I just can't
manage it all, even though I try! I'm desperate for
Your peace to reign in my day so I can thrive instead
of just try to survive. In Jesus' name I pray. Amen.*

# THE GIFT OF PEACE
# OF MIND AND HEART

———— Read John 14:1–27 ————

## Key Verse:

*"I am leaving you with a gift—peace of mind and
heart! And the peace I give isn't fragile like the peace
the world gives. So don't be troubled or afraid."*

JOHN 14:27 TLB

## Understand:

- Think about the worldly remedies you rely on when
  you're stressed out. Food? Shopping? Busyness?
  Pity parties? Netflix binge? Confess these to God
  and ask Him to help you think of His help first.

- If peace of mind and heart are gifts available to you
  through God, what might keep you from taking
  them?

*Apply:*

The ability for you to have peace of mind and an untroubled heart is a gift from the Lord. Scripture confirms these are available to every believer! So, knowing that, don't allow yourself to sit in stress and frustration any longer. Instead, grab hold of these gifts and harness the amazing benefits that come from them.

The world will always try to entice you with substitute fixes—ways to find temporary peace when you're stressed out—but they never compare to what God offers. The world's remedies are fragile and flimsy, often leaving you more stressed than before. But when you decide to lean into the Lord, you'll experience a sense of calm that will quiet your troubled heart. You'll have a confidence that's unmatched. And the ups and downs of life won't be able to take you out like in the past. Your heart will be peaceful despite it all.

*Pray:*

*God, forgive me for not trusting You enough. Forgive me for placing my faith in what the world offers. I'm grateful for the gift of peace in a stressful world, and I'm committed to placing my faith in You above all else. In Jesus' name I pray. Amen.*

# STANDING UP FOR
# WHAT'S RIGHT

──────── **Read Psalm 55:1–23** ────────

## *Key Verse*:

*Leave your troubles with the Lord, and he will defend you; he never lets honest people be defeated.*

PSALM 55:22 GNT

## *Understand*:

- What does it mean to you when God says He will never let honest people be defeated? How does that empower you? What situation does it bring to mind?

- Have you ever considered you may be feeling stress because you inserted yourself into a situation that He never asked you to join or in a way He never intended?

- What are the benefits of leaving your troubles with God?

*Apply:*

Standing up for what's right can be stressful because it's often unpopular. The reality is we live in a world where the moral fabric is being ripped apart right in front of us. People and policies have been on a mission to remove God's name from society. We're being told to accept things that are far from what we believe to be godly. And based on the overreactions we see when others are challenged, we're terrified to be the ones to stand up and speak out.

The best thing we can do when our stress is rising and our courage is waning is run to God. Scripture says He won't ever let honest people be defeated. So ask Him if you're to interject truth to a situation. Ask if He wants you to redirect someone making bad choices. If it's His will, you can trust God to give you the confidence and courage to do it.

*Pray:*

*God, I'm leaving my troubled heart with You and asking for a courageous one instead. The idea of speaking up for justice brings on stress, so I'm depending on You to direct me in the when and how as I follow Your lead. In Jesus' name I pray. Amen.*

# THE POWER OF A
# LIFE-GIVING WORD

————— Read Proverbs 12:13–28 —————

## *Key Verse*:

*Anxious fear brings depression, but a
life-giving word of encouragement can
do wonders to restore joy to the heart.*

PROVERBS 12:25 TPT

## *Understand*:

- Who are the people in your life that speak life-giving words of encouragement to you? Think back to how their words have helped you overcome stress.

- What are your thoughts on community? Can you see the benefits even when it's let you down in the past? What are they?

- What is God saying to you right now about certain relationships? What is your next right move?

*Apply:*

God made us to live in community. The reality is we need people, even though they drive us nuts at times. You're an introvert and think you don't have a huge need to be around family and friends? There is still no excuse. We're built for relationships, and every one of us stands to reap the beautiful benefits of them. And it's community done right that helps us live a less stressed life. There is great wisdom in knowing this.

When you're feeling anxious about your presentation, a timely *atta girl* helps you feel better. After a big fight, being reminded you're worthy of love restores peace. When you've had an epic parenting fail, hearing a good friend affirm your heart for your kids calms you down. Stress and anxiety may knock you to your knees, but a life-giving word of encouragement will help you stand tall again. And community delivers it powerfully.

*Pray:*

*God, thank You for community and the words
of encouragement they deliver to help combat
stress and anxiety. They are so good for my weary
heart. Help me see the wisdom in embracing
friends and family even when they've let me
down in the past. In Jesus' name I pray. Amen.*

# LET STRESS DRIVE
# YOU TO PRAYER

—————— Read Psalm 118:1–29 ——————

## *Key Verse:*

*In my distress I prayed to the Lord, and he answered
me and rescued me. He is for me! How can I be afraid?
What can mere man do to me? The Lord is on my
side; he will help me. Let those who hate me beware.*

PSALM 118:5–7 TLB

## *Understand:*

- Consider that since God already knows what's causing every bit of anxiety in your life and He understands every detail, He may be your best confidant.

- What would have to change for you to let God be your rescuer instead of anything the world has to offer?

- What role does fear of man play in your life?

## *Apply:*

No matter what is stressing you out, pray. When your test results show something you didn't expect, cry out to God. When the bills are piling up and you can't make ends meet, tell God about it. Every time your insecurities are triggered by something someone said, whisper a prayer to God. Regardless of who hurt your feelings, share it with the Lord. No matter what stress comes your way—and there may be many—let the Lord be your first stop.

The most potent remedy for a less stressed life is bringing God into those discouraging moments. Let Him be the One you run to the moment anxiety hits. The Lord has a perfect track record in your life, and that won't change. He's trustworthy and faithful. And believing God is on your side builds courage to withstand anything because you know He never loses; therefore, neither do you. Let stress drive you to prayer.

## *Pray:*

*God, grow my faith so I can trust You with the things that scare me and stress me out. I worry way too much, and it takes away my joy. Remind me that You're always on my side, especially when I let fear of man get in the way. You've never failed me, and You won't start now. In Jesus' name I pray. Amen.*

# YOU'RE NEVER ALONE

––––––– **Read Romans 8:24–39** –––––––

### *Key Verse:*

*So, what does all this mean? If God has deter-
mined to stand with us, tell me, who then could
ever stand against us? For God has proved his
love by giving us his greatest treasure, the gift
of his Son. And since God freely offered him
up as the sacrifice for us all, he certainly won't
withhold from us anything else he has to give.*
ROMANS 8:31–32 TPT

### *Understand:*

- Take inventory of the state of your relationships.
  Do you feel fulfilled by them? Alone in them? How
  do they affect your self-worth?

- Consider the connection between your relationships
  and your stress level. What patterns do you see?

- How does knowing you can never be alone affect
  you?

*Apply:*

Life can be volatile. There are seasons in relationships where the weight of worry feels too heavy. Sometimes friends abandon you, and your emotions are all stirred up. No matter the age of your children, being a mom can feel isolating when they choose rebellion, leaving you full of anxiety. And the pain of rejection in marriage is often unmatched. In those moments where you feel everyone is against you, remind yourself it isn't true. It may seem like the world is taking sides and you're left all alone, but God gave you Jesus as a gift. He also promised that His presence will be with you always, according to scripture.

These are the times you cling to your faith. This is when you saturate yourself in God's truths. When you choose to press close to the Lord, you will be fully aware of His calming presence. And stress will be replaced by peace.

*Pray:*

*God, thank You for promising to never leave me. Right now, I feel so lonely and unlovable. Please come close to me and remind me I am worthwhile. And when the world doesn't agree, remind me that You do. In Jesus' name I pray. Amen.*

# BLESSED FOR OBEDIENCE

----------- Read James 1:1–15 -----------

### *Key Verse*:

*Happy is the person who can hold up under the trials of life. At the right time, he'll know God's sweet approval and will be crowned with life. As God has promised, the crown awaits all who love Him.*
JAMES 1:12 VOICE

### *Understand*:

- What is your common response to the trials of life? Are they based in faith or fear? What needs to change?

- Did you realize God blesses obedience? Have you seen this play out in your life? In the life of someone else? What is the Holy Spirit speaking to you right now?

- Have you talked to the Lord about the things you're facing?

*Apply:*

It's hard to hold up under the trials of life. It takes strong faith to stay steady when everything around you seems to be falling apart. Sometimes life charges at you like a runaway locomotive, and you can't get out of the way. Be it bankruptcy, loss of a loved one, being laid off, failing out of school, discovering the betrayal, or a million other heartbreaks, it's easy to crumble under the weight of it all. And honestly, it's a common response for all of us.

But God has a different plan in mind. There's a beautiful reward waiting on the other side when you refuse to let the stressors of life keep you down. Not only will you find happiness and joy amid trials, but you'll feel God's approval in your spirit. Your faith will be recognized. So don't wait. Ask the Lord for strength and perseverance, and let His peace be what over-whelms you so stressful situations wash away instead of your hope.

*Pray:*

*God, thank You for rewarding my faith.*
*I appreciate that You understand the struggles*
*I face and the challenge obedience can be*
*when I'm feeling overwhelmed by life. Grow my*
*faith to trust You for the hope and healing I am*
*desperate for. In Jesus' name I pray. Amen.*

# STAYING PRESENT

---------- Read Matthew 6:19–34 ----------

## *Key Verse*:

*"Give your entire attention to what God is doing right now, and don't get worked up about what may or may not happen tomorrow. God will help you deal with whatever hard things come up when the time comes."*

MATTHEW 6:34 MSG

## *Understand*:

- Do you live in the present, or are you constantly thinking about the worries of tomorrow? What does that rob you of?

- Make a list of what's stressing you out about the future. Tell God about each struggle. Thank Him for His promise to help you handle hard things at the right time.

*Apply:*

One of the hardest things to do is stay present in today without letting our worry spill over to tomorrow. There are more than enough stressful situations to deal with in these twenty-four hours, amen? The Enemy would love nothing more than for us to look forward because he knows that's where he can interject fear. When we get too far ahead of ourselves and focus on the future, all we see are horrible outcomes and endings. We rarely project good things. And our worrying about tomorrow keeps us steeped in stress.

Ask God to help you be present in today. Set your sights on what needs your attention right now. Where do you need to make decisions? What issues do you need to be resolved? Who is asking for your help? Don't let the Enemy stress you out with tomorrow. God is already there, and you will be soon enough. Live these twenty-four hours with purpose and passion!

*Pray:*

*God, it is very hard for me to not worry about what's ahead. I see so many traps and pitfalls coming up, and I end up focusing my time trying to figure out ways to avoid them. It robs me of being present with those I love. And it keeps me from trusting You. Please help me stay present so I can live in obedience to Your plan, believing You'll help me at the right time. In Jesus' name I pray. Amen.*

# HOW TO LIVE
# BOLD AND STRONG

———— **Read Joshua 1:1–18** ————

## Key Verse:

*"Yes, be bold and strong! Banish fear
and doubt! For remember, the Lord your
God is with you wherever you go."*

JOSHUA 1:9 TLB

## Understand:

- What roles do fear and anxiety play in your life? Are they occasional struggles or ones you battle every day? What is God speaking to you about them?

- Do your actions reveal a belief that God will make up the difference and fill in the gap for you? In your opinion, is He trustworthy to help you be bold and fearless?

*Apply:*

The Word is clear that we're to be bold at all times. We're to be emotionally and mentally strong when hard things come our way. Rather than allow fear to take up any space in our day, we are to remove it so we are free. And doubt is to have no home in our heart. Does this feel impossible? Well, friend, it is. That's exactly why God promises to be with us. We need His presence to make this kind of living possible. And with the Lord's help, it is.

Life will never play fair, and there will always be reasons to be stressed out and worried. But your faith in God will give you the ability to weather any storm. Are you having a difficult time trusting Him? If you're struggling, ask Him to grow your faith. Every place you lack, He will replenish.

*Pray:*

*God, You ask hard things of me, and sometimes I wish you didn't. But in my pursuit to live a less stressed life, I realize how important a relationship with You is. You're the One who makes righteous living possible. You're the One who adds the "super" to my "natural" so I can walk it out. Thank You for Your presence in my life. I love You! In Jesus' name I pray. Amen.*

# THE STRESS OF HOSPITALITY

———————— Read Luke 10:25–42 ————————

## Key Verse:

*Martha was upset over all the work she had to do, so she came and said, "Lord, don't you care that my sister has left me to do all the work by myself? Tell her to come and help me!" The Lord answered her, "Martha, Martha! You are worried and troubled over so many things, but just one is needed. Mary has chosen the right thing, and it will not be taken away from her."*

LUKE 10:40–42 GNT

## Understand:

- What stands out in this story of Martha that challenges you?

- Can you relate to her feelings? Think back to the last time you felt burdened with hospitality. What was your response? How did you handle it? What could you have done differently?

*Apply:*

Aren't you thankful God shared Martha's story in the Bible? It shows how well He knows His daughters, doesn't it? This older sister was stressed out and ticked off because she was stuck in the kitchen. It seemed the chore of hospitality sat on her shoulders alone. Mary, the younger sister, abandoned her to sit with Jesus, and eventually Martha was unable to manage the anger and anxiety. Can you relate? Does her story bring up memories from your own life?

Taking on the responsibilities of hosting a group or an event is hard work. For some, it's one of the greatest joys. But for others, it stirs up all sorts of anxiety because there are so many moving parts. It can be stressful on many levels! One of the greatest lessons we can learn from Martha is to take those frustrations and fears right to the Lord. Tell Him what emotions you're battling. Ask for His help. Let the Lord be your go-to when the stress feels too overwhelming.

*Pray:*

*God, I don't want to be bitter as I bless others through hospitality. Help me choose to love with a servant's heart, and remind me to talk to You whenever stress and frustrations begin. In Jesus' name I pray. Amen.*

# THE WAY TO BE VICTORIOUS

—————— Read 1 Peter 5:1–14 ——————

## Key Verse:

*So bow down under God's strong hand; then when the time comes, God will lift you up. Since God cares for you, let Him carry all your burdens and worries. Most importantly, be disciplined and stay on guard. Your enemy the devil is prowling around outside like a roaring lion, just waiting and hoping for the chance to devour someone.*

1 PETER 5:6–8 VOICE

## Understand:

- Have you ever considered the role the devil plays to ruin your life? How does it make you feel to realize he is always looking for ways to bring discouragement? How does this change things for you?

- What keeps you from letting God carry your burdens and worries? What will you do differently moving forward?

*Apply:*

You have a real enemy in the devil. At every turn, his plans are to destroy and discourage you. He wants to turn your life upside down and inflict heartache whenever possible. The Word says he prowls around like a lion looking for opportunities to devour you. Not a pretty picture, friend. It's unsettling at best. And now you understand why stress and anxiety can be so difficult to manage.

But take heart! God will always make a way for you to be victorious. In those moments, surrender every fear and anxiety to Him. Tell God what's on your heart. And when you do, He'll not only give you strength to rise up in confidence but will also remove burdens weighing you down. The Enemy will target you, but your faith is a shield. It'll protect you from his schemes. So, friend, be quick to use it when stress comes on.

*Pray:*

*God, I didn't realize the devil was so interested in ruining my life. It makes sense now. And it makes me see the vital importance of letting You carry the weight of my stress because he is no match for You. And I know I am safe in Your arms. In Jesus' name I pray. Amen.*

# HOW TO LIVE WITH PASSION

———— **Read Hebrews 12:1–17** ————

## *Key Verse*:

*As for us, we have all of these great witnesses
who encircle us like clouds. So we must let go of
every wound that has pierced us and the sin we
so easily fall into. Then we will be able to run life's
marathon race with passion and determination, for
the path has been already marked out before us.*

HEBREWS 12:1 TPT

## *Understand*:

- Take inventory of your heart. Are you stressed?
  Are you holding on to unforgiveness? How is it
  affecting you right now?

- What would need to happen for you to be able to
  live life with passion? Where does God fit into that?

## *Apply*:

When we choose to hold onto times we've been wounded by others, it's bondage. Unforgiveness is a nasty habit that robs us of freedom and causes us to replay the hurtful situation in our mind. It keeps us in a perpetual state of stress as we relive the offense on the regular. And when we choose this kind of living, it effectively shuts us down. We don't live with passion. We live with pain.

Don't ever forget God has set you up for a life of passion and courage. He set a path for you to walk. Sitting in hurt feelings and staying stuck in your pain keeps you too anxious to follow God's lead. And you'll miss His blessings along the way. It's not easy to keep moving forward when you've been knocked to your knees. Ask the Lord to heal your heart and then point you in the right direction.

## *Pray*:

*God, I confess I hold onto old wounds too tightly.
I've been deeply hurt, and letting go of the offense
would feel like they've won. But I realize now
it's what's kept me from living with passion and
courage. Please heal my heart so I can follow
You with my life. In Jesus' name I pray. Amen.*

# TRUSTING GOD MORE

—————— **Read Proverbs 3:1–20** ——————

## Key Verse:

*Trust in the Lord completely, and do not rely on your own opinions. With all your heart rely on him to guide you, and he will lead you in every decision you make. Become intimate with him in whatever you do, and he will lead you wherever you go.*

PROVERBS 3:5–6 TPT

## Understand:

- What does it mean to trust in the Lord completely? How are you doing with that?

- Be honest. Whom do you rely on the most for guidance and wisdom?

- What keeps you from following God? Do you not hear Him? Is His path scary? Is it stressful to trust an unknown future you can't see? How do you reconcile this?

*Apply:*

We get into trouble when we choose to rely on ourselves over God. When we decide we know more or know better, it's a recipe for disaster. The truth is that we're smart and we've lived enough life to make wise choices. We may be surrounded by people who give us solid counsel, but no one is smarter than God.

Are you struggling in marriage? Unsure about how to parent your child? Stressed about big financial woes? Anxious over a health issue? Scared about the future? Let God be the voice you listen to. Read His Word as you wait for His leading. Talk to Him but be sure to listen as well. And be aware when the Holy Spirit gives you a gut feeling. If you'll pursue it and have patience, God will lead you in every decision you must make. Let Him be the One to guide you through life.

*Pray:*

*God, grow my trust muscle so I can confidently follow You without fear. I confess it's stressful to let You guide me because I'm unsure if I'm hearing Your voice or my own. Give me assurance as I choose to rely on You over me or anyone else. I want to follow your lead no matter what. In Jesus' name I pray. Amen.*

# YOU CAN'T MESS IT UP

———— Read Psalm 103:1–22 ————

### Key Verse:

*He is merciful and tender toward those who don't deserve it; he is slow to get angry and full of kindness and love. He never bears a grudge, nor remains angry forever. He has not punished us as we deserve for all our sins, for his mercy toward those who fear and honor him is as great as the height of the heavens above the earth.*

PSALM 103:8–11 TLB

### Understand:

- Think about who you believe God to be? Is He loving and kind? Is He angry and full of wrath? How does today's verse line up with your thoughts?

- With a heart of gratitude, confess your shortcomings to God and thank Him for not holding them against you. Sit with that powerful truth and let Him remove any guilt, shame, or fear.

*Apply:*

Sometimes we get stressed, thinking we've angered God and ruined our chances with Him. We worry we have done the one thing that will cause Him to walk away. Because we have experienced that kind of abandonment and rejection from those around us, it's easy to think God will react the same way. But that's simply not true. Not by a mile.

God's Word is clear that He is merciful, even when we don't deserve it. His temper is slow to rise, unlike ours. And rather than lash out or make us pay for our transgressions, He chooses to show unmatched kindness. Take a deep breath and soak in the truth that God doesn't hold grudges. You can mess up and still be loved. Always forgiven. And there is nothing you can do to change that.

*Pray:*

*God, You are amazing. I don't understand how You love me, especially with the ways I've messed up. I confess my stress and fear of You turning away from me. But now my heart is full of joy to know that's not the kind of God You are. I love You! In Jesus' name I pray. Amen.*

# THE POWERFUL EFFECT OF GOD'S LOVE

---------------- Read 1 John 4:7–21 ----------------

## *Key Verse:*

*God is love. When we take up permanent residence
in a life of love, we live in God and God lives in us.
This way, love has the run of the house, becomes
at home and mature in us, so that we're free of
worry on Judgment Day—our standing in the world
is identical with Christ's. There is no room in love
for fear. Well-formed love banishes fear. Since fear
is crippling, a fearful life—fear of death, fear of
judgment—is one not yet fully formed in love.*
1 JOHN 4:17–18 MSG

## *Understand:*

- Consider the connection between God and love.
  How do these two intertwine in a powerful way and
  benefit you?

- How does God's love banish fear and stress?

34

*Apply:*

It's difficult to grasp the depth and breadth of love God has for us. But when (and if) we truly embrace it as best we can, regardless of our human condition, it changes how we think about the day we will stand in front of God and give an account for how we've lived. When we allow His love to settle on us and bring about the necessary maturity, we don't have to live with any stress of that moment in time.

You can also let that truth affect your life in the here and now. God says there's no room for fear when His love is present. There is no space for stress. There's no acreage for anxiety. Choose to let that be how you approach life. Ask God to make His promises come alive in you. And dare to believe there's nothing that can separate you from Him.

*Pray:*

*God, thank You for the transformative power of Your love. Let it infiltrate my life so I am able to live without stress and fear right now, as well as on judgement day. Your perfect love allows me to be free in every way! In Jesus' name I pray. Amen.*

# THE CALL TO RADICAL TRUST

—— **Read Luke 12:13–31** ——

## Key Verse:

*Then Jesus said to the disciples, "And so I tell you not to worry about the food you need to stay alive or about the clothes you need for your body. Life is much more important than food, and the body much more important than clothes."*
LUKE 12:22–23 GNT

## Understand:

- Why do you think Jesus would ask the disciples to not worry about basic human needs that were important to them? What does this tell you?

- What place of lacking is stressing you out right now? Have you talked to God about it more than you've worried about it? What needs to change?

*Apply:*

Jesus was clear when He told the disciples to exercise trust over stress. He offered a radical perspective to a common concern. And imagine the shift in their thinking when He insisted they need not worry about the basic things in life—things we all worry about. Stressing out about these types of necessities are about as normal as normal gets. Amen? Jesus was redirecting their focus.

What are the basics you're worried about today? Are you struggling to pay bills? Do your kids need school supplies or team uniforms at your cost? Is your refrigerator empty? Maybe God is trying to redirect your focus from yourself to the One who is able and willing to meet every need. Maybe He is about to grow your faith through radical trust. Talk to God about where you're worried, and believe He will provide in supernatural ways.

*Pray:*

*God, this is a hard command because there are so many needs in my life. It feels silly to let go of stress and striving and trust You to meet my needs. I know this isn't a call to sit around in inactivity but rather to listen for Your leading and watch for Your provision. Grow my faith so I can choose trust in You over worry every time. In Jesus' name I pray. Amen.*

# IN LACK AND ABUNDANCE

———— Read Philippians 4:1–23 ————

## Key Verse:

*I know what it means to lack, and I know what it means to experience overwhelming abundance. For I'm trained in the secret of overcoming all things, whether in fullness or in hunger. And I find that the strength of Christ's explosive power infuses me to conquer every difficulty.*

PHILIPPIANS 4:12–13 TPT

## Understand:

- Think about the times you lack and the times of abundance. How do they affect your stress levels?

- Do you ask God to display His power in your life? Do you truly believe it will empower you through hard seasons?

## *Apply:*

So much of our stress comes from thinking we don't have enough. In our minds, the more we have the better. We equate plenty with comfort, and in our mind, comfort is key for keeping our stress levels low. At least that's what we often believe. But the reality is that nothing earthly can satisfy the deep needs in our soul. God is the only One who can help us steady ourselves in troubled times.

Friend, things won't ever bring true contentment—at least not for long. They won't help you win or give you strength. They won't keep stress at bay. Instead, they'll offer only empty promises. And like Paul, it's important you realize it's Jesus alone who assures you'll be an overcomer. When you access His power—be it in lack or in abundance—you'll be divinely infused with courage and confidence to face every difficult circumstance that comes your way.

## *Pray:*

*God, I think I've looked for comfort and confidence in all the wrong things. Forgive me for chasing after abundance rather than You. Forgive me for complaining in my seasons of lack instead of asking You for help. I know now that it's Christ's explosive power that will infuse me to face the trials of life. It's Him alone. In Jesus' name I pray. Amen.*

# WHEN THE CRISIS COMES

—————— Read Proverbs 24:1–34 ——————

## Key Verse:

*If you fall apart during a crisis, then you
weren't very strong to begin with.*
PROVERBS 24:10 VOICE

## Understand:

- Think back to the last time you faced a crisis. What was your response? Whom did you run to? How well did your faith hold up?

- In your opinion, how does a relationship with God help when life hits you in the gut?

- Where does your strength come from? Would others see that in you?

## Apply:

Today's verse may seem harsh, but sometimes we need a stark wake-up call to open our eyes. This is one of those times. Friend, if your desire is to live a less stressed life, then you must anchor your faith tightly to God. He has to be your default button. The Lord needs to be the first stop every time because deep down you truly believe He's all you need. You have to believe without fail that God has every answer and solution.

Your responses will always reveal your level of faith. It's a choice to trust the Lord when everything around you is falling apart. It takes discipline to make Him be the One you turn to first. And this is made possible through time with Him. The more time you spend with God, the more you trust Him. And the greater the trust, the stronger your faith.

## Pray:

*God, I confess I fall apart pretty easily. In my stress and worry, I feel so weak. I am often paralyzed and ineffective. And honestly, it's a sad revelation because I didn't connect the dots. But starting today, I'm committed to deepening my relationship with You so when a crisis does hit, I have a strong faith to face what's ahead of me rather than crumble in anxiety. I know that with You, I am able to navigate every hard season or situation. Thank You! In Jesus' name I pray. Amen.*

# REMOVING THE STRESS OF OBEYING

Read Luke 6:27–48

## Key Verse:

*But all those who come and listen and obey me*
*are like a man who builds a house on a strong*
*foundation laid upon the underlying rock. When*
*the floodwaters rise and break against the*
*house, it stands firm, for it is strongly built.*
LUKE 6:47–48 TLB

## Understand:

- Think about the words *obey* and *submit*. What kind of emotions do they stir in you? Where does that response come from?

- Compare your feelings triggered by those words with God's reasoning for asking them. How do they differ? Why can you trust Him?

*Apply:*

We often hear the word *submit* and freak out. Sometimes there are so many negatives attached to it, we can't get past them. Maybe there are memories of real trauma the word conjures up. Maybe you were shamed growing up because the idea of obedience was misused by your parents. Or maybe it makes you feel weak and unimportant. When we feel forced to obey and surrender our thoughts or desires, it can bring up stress and fear. But it's important to remember God would never ask anything of you that would stir those feelings in negative ways.

When the Lord asks for obedience, it's for your benefit. He knows surrendering your will to His will only strengthens you. It will bring peace. It will keep you from drowning in difficulties. It will make you wise and resolved and courageous. It will create a firm foundation of faith in your life. And best of all, stress and fear won't rule your heart.

*Pray:*

*God, I confess that the idea of obedience is a hard one for me. There's a lot of baggage that comes with it. Please whisper confidence into my heart so I can trust You as I choose to submit my will to Yours. The truth is that You're always trustworthy; therefore, my capitulation is always a safe decision. Be my foundation so I can weather every storm. In Jesus' name I pray. Amen.*

# THERE IN A MINUTE

— Read Psalm 94:1–23 —

### *Key Verse*:

*Who stood up for me against the wicked? Who took my side against evil workers? If GOD hadn't been there for me, I never would have made it. The minute I said, "I'm slipping, I'm falling," your love, GOD, took hold and held me fast. When I was upset and beside myself, you calmed me down and cheered me up.*

PSALM 94:16–19 MSG

### *Understand*:

- Think about your support system. Are they available when you need them? Do they have your best in mind?

- Is it possible you put too much faith in your friends and family and end up disappointed when they don't meet your needs?

- What are the benefits of holding on to God over anyone else?

*Apply:*

We can begin to feel so anxious when it seems no one is standing up for us. When we are a solo act in times of trouble, all sorts of fears appear. Honestly, no one likes to navigate choppy waters alone. So when the job we love is being eliminated, or our perfect health takes an unexpected turn, or our husband walks out on our twenty-year marriage, remember God has promised to be right there. The minute we cry out for help, we will be held.

Because He created you, He knows exactly what makes you tick. He understands what you need better than you. He sees your fear. He sees the stress and worry. And in God's infinite wisdom, He has a plan to calm your anxious heart and put a smile on your face. With this promise, why let anyone else try to make you feel better?

*Pray:*

*God, I am so grateful for my community because they love me as well as they can. But the truth is that no one can take Your place. You understand those deep places in my heart that need divine intervention. When I cry for You, be quick. In those moments, I desperately need what only You can offer. In Jesus' name I pray. Amen.*

# GOD WANTS YOUR FAITH

—————— Read Exodus 14:1–21 ——————

## Key Verse:

*Moses spoke to the people: "Don't be afraid. Stand firm and watch GOD do his work of salvation for you today. Take a good look at the Egyptians today for you're never going to see them again. GOD will fight the battle for you. And you? You keep your mouths shut!"*
EXODUS 14:13–14 MSG

## Understand:

- What scares you about trusting God to fight on your behalf? Do you struggle with unbelief that He can or will?

- Where do you feel surrounded by enemies right now? How are you coping? What needs to change?

## Apply:

Sometimes in our stress, we go into overdrive trying to fix things ourselves. We become overcontrolling in our pursuit of managing the situation. Other times we shut down and avoid anything that might pump more anxiety into the situation. We feel powerless. But God wants us to stand unafraid, confident of His deliverance.

In today's verse, the Israelites had just walked away from slavery in Egypt and were literally stuck between Pharaoh's army and the Red Sea. They were trapped. Unless God showed up, they'd die one way or the other. In their fear, it's fair to assume some wanted to try to fix the situation while others wanted to hide. The Lord, however, wanted their faith. He wants that from you too. In those tough times when you feel stressed and surrounded by enemies, stand firm and watch God battle for you.

## Pray:

*God, I feel stuck. There doesn't seem to be a way out of this mess. I've tried to fix things on my own but failed. I've cowered in fear so many times it's embarrassing. But the stress remains intact, and I'm overwhelmed by it all. Increase my faith in Your promised deliverance so I can stand strong, trusting that You will fight on my behalf. In Jesus' name I pray. Amen.*

# THE STRESS TO SATISFY

—————— **Read Hebrews 13:1–25** ——————

## *Key Verse*:

*Keep your lives free from the love of money, and be
satisfied with what you have. For God has said,
"I will never leave you; I will never abandon you."
Let us be bold, then, and say, "The Lord is my helper,
I will not be afraid. What can anyone do to me?"*
HEBREWS 13:5–6 GNT

## *Understand*:

- We all want to feel satisfied in life. What does that
  look like for you? Where does your contentment
  come from?

- When God says He will never leave or abandon you,
  how does that land in your heart? Does it bring
  peace? Is it a neutral feeling?

- What is the Holy Spirit speaking to you right now?

## *Apply:*

Few things cause more stress than money, and with good reason. There are natural consequences that come from our inability to pay a bill, and falling behind quickly increases our debt load. We stress as we try to keep up with those around us, spending over our limit on the regular. And if we're not careful, our craving for *things* will become the god we worship.

God repeatedly tells us in His Word to be satisfied with what we have—one of those being His presence. He knows it's a guaranteed stress buster because when we stop striving and choose contentment instead, it's peaceful. We can relax and not be hyperfocused on money. And that decision directly impacts our faith because we realize God is enough. So the next time you feel the urge to want more, want bigger, or want better, sit with the Lord and ask Him to satisfy your heart's desire with more of Him.

## *Pray:*

*God, I confess my need for more. I confess my love of money. I confess my struggle with jealousy and envy, unable to keep up with others. Thank You for understanding this and reminding me of your constant presence in my life. You're the reason I can stop striving and be at peace. You're why I can rest. In Jesus' name I pray. Amen.*

# WHEN YOU NEED REFRESHMENT

―――――――――― Read Isaiah 55:1–13 ――――――――――

## Key Verse:

*"Listen! Are you thirsty for more? Come to the refreshing waters and drink. Even if you have no money, come, buy, and eat. Yes, come and buy all the wine and milk you desire—it won't cost a thing. Why spend your hard-earned money on something that can't nourish you or work so hard for something that can't satisfy? So listen carefully to me and you'll enjoy a sumptuous feast, delighting in the finest of food."*

ISAIAH 55:1–2 TPT

## Understand:

- What are you thirsty for? Love? Attention? Validation? Acceptance? Hope?

- Compare and contrast what the world offers you and what God promises. What are the most notable differences? How should you respond?

## Apply:

Everything good comes from God. He's the only One who can quench your thirst for love. He will fulfill your desire to belong. God is the One who will meet every emotional and physical need—even the unspoken ones. He will remove the stress and fear that fuel lies whispered into your spirit saying you're worthless. And all it will cost you is faith.

As women, we have unique needs. God made us with a beautiful complexity that many use against us. Rather than embrace who we are, they criticize us. They tell us we're too much or too little. They call us high maintenance. They say we're exhausting. But God calls us to Him for validation. His arms are open wide. So set aside those earthly stressors and let the Lord reassure you that you're perfect in His eyes. Let Him refresh and nourish your spirit.

## Pray:

*God, help me remember that You are the only One who can bring lasting refreshment to my stressed-out spirit. I may look to other places and to other people, but they will never offer lasting hope. Thank You for making me complex and seeing it as beautiful. Don't let me give credence to anyone who turns that into something negative. In Jesus' name I pray. Amen.*

# THE CONNECTION BETWEEN STRESS AND SLEEPLESSNESS

---------- **Read Psalm 16:1–11** ----------

## *Key Verse:*

*The wise counsel GOD gives when I'm awake
is confirmed by my sleeping heart. Day and
night I'll stick with GOD; I've got a good
thing going and I'm not letting go.*

PSALM 16:7–8 MSG

## *Understand:*

- Think about the connection between stress and sleeplessness in your life. What does this look like for you?

- What would a dose of divine wisdom regarding that troubling situation you're battling do to help a night of restless sleep?

## *Apply:*

Worry and stress during the day make for a horrible night's sleep. When you're stressed about the upcoming interview, it's hard to sleep. When a difficult conversation is right around the corner, you're up all night rehearsing. When someone is struggling, you toss and turn in worry. The problem comes from an unwillingness to let it go. You stay stirred up with anxiety. But, friend, is God in the mix? Give your worries to Him so you can sleep.

Let Him be your wise counsel. If you need perspective, ask for it. If you need clarification, tell Him why. If discernment is what you're lacking, pray about it. Be actively engaging with God through the day so your mind and body can rest at night. Stick with Him for wisdom over anyone or anything else. Because when you let the Lord into those stressful situations that tug on your heart, He will bring peace and a sense of calm so you can rest.

## *Pray:*

*God, listen to me as I unpack my restless heart.
Let my confession during the day trigger a
restful night's sleep. Speak Your wisdom and
discernment into my spirit, bringing a revelation
of Your presence in my struggle. Help me trust
You over all else. In Jesus' name I pray. Amen.*

# WHEN THE FUTURE LOOKS SCARY

——— Read Jeremiah 29:1–23 ———

### Key Verse:

*"For I know the plans I have for you," says the Eternal, "plans for peace, not evil, to give you a future and hope—never forget that. At that time, you will call out for Me, and I will hear. You will pray, and I will listen. You will look for Me intently, and you will find Me."*
JEREMIAH 29:11–13 VOICE

### Understand:

- How does it make you feel to know God can see your entire future? Do your thoughts and actions line up together?

- What does it mean to call out for, pray to, and look for God *intently*? And what might you find when you do?

## *Apply*:

Sometimes we get super stressed about the future. When we look down the road, what we usually predict is terribleness. We see the worst possible outcomes. We decide every ending is horrible. And we're left stressed out and scared. God knows your future. When He thought you up, God decided your whole life from beginning to end. And scripture says the plans are for peace over evil, giving you a sense of hope for what's ahead.

In those moments—when all you see ahead is doom and gloom—call out to God for His perspective. Talk to Him in prayer and tell Him your worries. Unpack every fear and concern. Ask for confidence in His plan. God says when you seek Him out for help, you'll find Him. Have faith as you cry out, waiting to hear His still, small voice speak truth and life into your stressed-out and weary soul.

## *Pray*:

*God, it's comforting to know You planned a hope-filled future for me. That means when I feel stressed about what's ahead, I can talk to You because You're already aware. Even more, when I feel lost and overwhelmed and call out for Your help, it will come. When I pray, You will answer. And when I seek You out, I will always find You. What an awesome God! In Jesus' name I pray. Amen.*

# BUT GOD

Read John 16:1–33

### Key Verse:

*I have told you these things so that you will be whole
and at peace. In this world, you will be plagued
with times of trouble, but you need not fear;
I have triumphed over this corrupt world order.*

JOHN 16:33 VOICE

### Understand:

- How does knowing you will certainly face times of trouble help you manage the ups and downs of life?

- What does it look like to be whole and at peace?

- What does God mean when He says He has "triumphed" over the world?

## Apply:

Times of trouble are to be expected. At some point, we will all face seasons of stress and worry no matter how much we try to avoid them. No doubt, relationships will be strained. Divorces will happen. We will lose loved ones. Bullies will prevail. Bankruptcies will come to pass. Infertility will be a struggle. Insecurities will get triggered. Kids will challenge your patience. And the list goes on. This life will be hard, *but God.*

Those two simple words are anything but simple. They are beautifully complex and full of power and promise. They bring hope to the weary and courage to the cowardly. They remind you that your circumstances are no match for God because He will triumph over anything this corrupt world conjures up. And since the Lord is fully in the mix of your mess, these two words—*but God*—help melt the stress and anxiety that comes from an unknown future.

## Pray:

*God, why am I always surprised when times of trouble come my way? I know Your Word says to expect it, but it catches me off guard every time and destabilizes my heart. It stresses me out and scares me! Help me remember that because of You I can find victory in life. You've already overcome the world and all its corruption. My job is to press into that truth and trust You as I walk it out in real time. Please bolster my confidence and courage. In Jesus' name I pray. Amen.*

# FEAR IS NOT FROM GOD

—— Read 2 Timothy 1:1–18 ——

## Key Verse:

*I'm writing to encourage you to fan into a flame and rekindle the fire of the spiritual gift God imparted to you when I laid my hands upon you. For God will never give you the spirit of fear, but the Holy Spirit who gives you mighty power, love, and self-control.*

2 TIMOTHY 1:6–7 TPT

## Understand:

- What fresh revelation did you get from today's verse?

- How does reading about how fear isn't from God challenge your way of thinking?

- In your opinion, how do the Spirit's power, love, and self-control work together to benefit you?

*Apply:*

In those moments when you feel an overwhelming sense of fear and stress, remember neither are from God. When your confidence has been shaken to the core, He had nothing to do with it. Every time you're overcome with worry, don't point fingers at the Lord. Let this truth sink deep because it's imperative you know this for a fact. He will never scare you into obedience or stress you to the point of turning to Him. God won't be the initiator. Those aren't His ways.

Instead, notice in today's scripture what He does give you. Through His Spirit, you have access to mighty power, love, and self-control. These work together in powerful ways, allowing you to find courage for the battle and peace through it. Living in a state of stress is unhealthy on every level, and it's not God's best for you. So grab onto these gifts and activate them so you don't crumble under the weight of worry.

*Pray:*

*God, what a relief to know fear isn't in Your playbook. And when life storms hit hard, help me remember being stressed and worried doesn't have to be my response. You're a loving God who willingly and generously gives power, love, and self-control to those who ask. Remind me to cling to those as they'll help me overcome any fear I may be facing. In Jesus' name I pray. Amen.*

# LETTING GOD HAVE
# THE LAST WORD

## Read Proverbs 16:1–33

### Key Verse:

*Mortals make elaborate plans, but GOD has the last word. Humans are satisfied with whatever looks good; GOD probes for what is good. Put GOD in charge of your work, then what you've planned will take place.*

PROVERBS 16:1–3 MSG

### Understand:

- Think about how connected you are to your work and ideas. Is there flexibility in them? Are you rigid in your ways?

- What would have to change for you to let God have the last word in your plans?

- What is the Holy Spirit saying to you right now?

*Apply:*

What if rather than stress because your well-thought out plans aren't panning out you chose to trust the Lord instead? Think about how this decision would reduce your level of anxiety. You'd be able to pivot and be flexible. It would grow your faith as you truste God to work it out.

Friend, the Lord gave you a creative mind on purpose. He fitted you with grand ideas and the ability to organize, but He wants to be part of it. Inviting God into the process on the front end will help alleviate stress on the back end. Be patient and give Him time to speak into your work. Ask Him to make your plans align with His will. And when you decide to let God have the last word or change things up if He sees fit, it sets you up to move forward without anxiety.

*Pray:*

*God, I want to give You the last word in my plans.*
*I want Your will to matter more than my own.*
*Help me align my heart to Your ways. Help me*
*surrender my ideas to Yours. I choose to trust*
*You every day. In Jesus' name I pray. Amen.*

# TRUSTING OVER STRESSING

——————— Read Psalm 37:1–40 ———————

### Key Verse:

*Stop your anger! Turn off your wrath. Don't
fret and worry—it only leads to harm. For the
wicked shall be destroyed, but those who trust
the Lord shall be given every blessing.*

PSALM 37:8–9 TLB

### Understand:

- In your opinion, how do fret and worry lead to harm? Have you seen that play out in your own life?

- How do you need God to bless your situation right now? Are you trusting Him rather than stressing out?

## *Apply:*

When we get stressed, so often our next reaction is anger. There are times our temper is the first response, but most of the time it's our second. Think about it. When we are embarrassed, we often get mad. When we're anxious, we snap at those we love in frustration. When we are worrying, we are usually short tempered. When we're full of fear, we are cranky and intolerant. Maybe that's why today's verse addresses the response of anger and wrath first.

Let's choose to be women whose first reaction is faith. When everything seems to be falling apart around us, let's be quick to turn our eyes to God. Trusting leads to blessing, and who doesn't need that? Let stress drive you to your knees so the Lord can give you the ability to stand strong in your faith.

## *Pray:*

*God, I confess that I often let anger get the best of me. It is my second response to stress and fear, and I'm just now making that connection. Thank You for this revelation! Would You help me be quick to activate my faith rather than marinate in anger and wrath? You are trustworthy in every situation, and I am committed to choosing You over any and every joy-draining emotion. They are dead ends that cause nothing but pain. In Jesus' name I pray. Amen.*

# THE BENEFIT OF FLEXIBILITY

———————— Read Habakkuk 3:1–19 ————————

## *Key Verse*:

*Even though the fig trees have no fruit and no grapes grow on the vines, even though the olive crop fails and the fields produce no grain, even though the sheep all die and the cattle stalls are empty, I will still be joyful and glad, because the LORD God is my savior. The Sovereign LORD gives me strength. He makes me sure-footed as a deer and keeps me safe on the mountains.*

HABAKKUK 3:17–19 GNT

## *Understand*:

- Reword the first sentence in today's verse, adding your own *even though* situations. How does this help alleviate stress in your situation?

- Would others in your life say you're rigid or flexible? What needs to change?

*Apply:*

If we would adapt the same kind of steady faith modeled in today's verse, we could keep stress at bay. We battle anxiety most when we feel things are out of our hands. When our best efforts don't seem to be good enough, our stress level is off the chart. We want to be in full control, so all outcomes are predictable. And too often, we try to manage anyone and anything so they can be. But if we are going to be women living less stressed lives, we need to trust God the most.

Trusting Him helps us become flexible and willing to switch to plan B, if necessary. It takes the rigidity out of the situation so we can give God's plan room to bloom without our interference. And in the end, it helps remind us that it's all about the Lord. He is why we can live with joy. He is how we have strength. He is who removes the stress.

*Pray:*

*God, I want to have "even though" faith so I can be flexible as I trust Your will and way. Give me a courageous desire to pivot and shift as You lead. I don't want to live filled with stress, especially knowing that trusting You offers joy instead. In Jesus' name I pray. Amen.*

# PEACE IN EVERY CIRCUMSTANCE

—————— Read 2 Thessalonians 3:1–16 ——————

## Key Verse:

*Now, may the Lord himself, the Lord of
peace, pour into you his peace in every
circumstance and in every possible way.
The Lord's tangible presence be with you all.*
2 THESSALONIANS 3:16 TPT

## Understand:

- What is the difference between the peace God offers and the peace you find from the world? Which do you seek most?

- Consider every circumstance that feels undone in your life. Where is stress thriving? What is the key to finding rest and comfort?

*Apply:*

God promises to give you peace in every circumstance you must face. When you're grieving the loss of someone you dearly loved. When you are struggling to find the confidence to take the next step. When relationships are stressing you out. When you feel overwhelmed by decisions. In those lonely seasons that feel endless. When the state of the world scares you. When you don't feel smart enough. These are times ripe for stress, but the Lord made a way to find comfort in and through them.

Take a moment to realize that God Himself—the One who created the heavens and the earth—wants to pour His peace into your situation. Because He loves you so much, God promises to be with you so you're never alone. Friend, let Him be the One to settle the anxiousness that steals your joy.

*Pray:*

*God, remind me to ask for Your peace over anything the world offers. I don't need false hope or short-term solutions. Instead, I crave the peace that endures. You know every situation I'm battling right now, and I'm feeling stirred up and stressed out. Please meet me in it. Settle my anxious heart. Give me hope and joy. All I need is You. In Jesus' name I pray. Amen.*

# THE NEED FOR RENEWAL

———————— Read Romans 12:1–21 ————————

## *Key Verse:*

*Do not allow this world to mold you in its own image. Instead, be transformed from the inside out by renewing your mind. As a result, you will be able to discern what God wills and whatever God finds good, pleasing, and complete.*
ROMANS 12:2 VOICE

## *Understand:*

- What does it mean to be transformed from the inside out? How does that help with stress?

- What are things you can do to make sure the world doesn't mold you into its image? How does God help?

*Apply:*

Sometimes we mistakenly decide stress is a good thing—a badge of honor, of sorts. Have you ever felt accomplished because life was so busy, even though it felt overwhelming? Have you felt pride as you bragged about having so much to deal with? Do you thrive in chaotic situations and therefore try to stay in one? These are not God's hopes for you. Instead, these are ideals courtesy of the world.

Every one of us needs a renewing of the mind because we all fall prey to the world's way. How can we not? So it's important we ask the Lord to transform our thinking to align with His. When we think about it, we know stress isn't His plan. He doesn't want us to live in fear. Worry and anxiety aren't in His playbook. And even more, these keep us from knowing God's will for our lives.

*Pray:*

*God, I'm asking You to transform me from the inside out, so I don't follow the world's direction. Renew my mind in every way so I'm focused on what You find to be good, pleasing, and complete. I want my heart to seek after You alone. I want my life to reflect Your kindness and goodness. And I want my words and actions to point others to You in heaven. In Jesus' name I pray. Amen.*

# THE ANTIDOTE
# TO GULLIBILITY

———————— Read Romans 16:17–27 ————————

## Key Verse:

*And so while there has never been any question
about your honesty in these matters—I couldn't be
more proud of you!—I want you also to be smart,
making sure every "good" thing is the real thing.
Don't be gullible in regard to smooth-talking evil.
Stay alert like this, and before you know it the God
of peace will come down on Satan with both feet,
stomping him into the dirt. Enjoy the best of Jesus!*
ROMANS 16:19–20 MSG

## Understand:

- How does discernment help to overcome gullibil-
  ity? Where is God in that process?

- What are some practical ways your faith will help
  you become alert? How will they relieve stress?

## Apply:

Are you gullible, easily swayed by others? Don't beat yourself up, friend. It doesn't mean you're weak or lack smarts. Many of us choose to think the best of others, and so we do. Sometimes, however, it gets us into trouble. We end up disillusioned and stressed out as we discover we've been had. And the Enemy takes a bow. But take heart because God always makes a way.

Scripture tells us we can ask for His wisdom and that doing so will help us recognize what is true. We can ask for discernment to know what is right. And we can ask for the Holy Spirit in us to alert us to what is real. These requests keep us from trusting in the wrong things and wrong people, thereby insulating us from stress. And that act of faith allows us to stay in the peace of Jesus as He contends with the Enemy.

## Pray:

*God, help me be wise. Bless me with discernment so I know what is right and wrong. Let me be quick to see when I'm believing untruths. I want to be alert and focused so I can follow Your ways alone. In Jesus' name I pray. Amen.*

# DE-STRESSING BY BLESSING

———————— Read Isaiah 58:1-14 ————————

### *Key Verse:*

*Feed the hungry! Help those in trouble! Then your light will shine out from the darkness, and the darkness around you shall be as bright as day. And the Lord will guide you continually, and satisfy you with all good things, and keep you healthy too; and you will be like a well-watered garden, like an ever-flowing spring.*

ISAIAH 58:10-11 TLB

### *Understand:*

- Think back to times you've volunteered. How did it affect your attitude about struggles in your own life?

- Based on today's passage of scripture, what are the benefits of turning your focus from yourself to others?

## *Apply:*

One way to help relieve stress is to take the focus off yourself. When we face difficulties, it's easy and natural to become so absorbed with our own battle that we don't see the battles of others around us. It's unintentional selfishness that robs us of perspective. But turning our eyes outward to see the needs of others brings a bounty of blessing on them and yourself. It brings a much-needed shift for your heart.

Your kindness will shine His light into dark situations. And knowing your time and effort has helped others diminishes the weight of your own worry. When talking to God about the stress you're facing, ask Him to bring opportunities for you to focus on others as well. Look for ways of de-stressing by blessing, and feel the anxiety melt away when you do.

## *Pray:*

*God, I confess that I become selfish in my distress because I'm preoccupied by the personal circumstances I'm having to manage. When facing fear and worry, I usually only focus on myself. Please open my heart to meeting the needs of others and being sensitive to their situations. Let that refocus bring peace to me in meaningful ways. In Jesus' name I pray. Amen.*

# FROM STRANGLING STRESS TO PERFECT PEACE

---- Read Psalm 34:1–22 ----

## Key Verse:

*GOD met me more than halfway, he freed me from my anxious fears. Look at him; give him your warmest smile. Never hide your feelings from him. When I was desperate, I called out, and GOD got me out of a tight spot.*

PSALM 34:4–6 MSG

## Understand:

- List out your anxious fears and share them with God.

- In the past, how have you sought freedom from stress? What are your go-to remedies for relief? How does God fit into them?

## *Apply:*

We all face anxious fears that hold us in bondage and keep us from living in confidence. Maybe when walking into the courtroom to finalize the divorce. Maybe when sitting down to have a dreaded conversation. Maybe when the debt collector sends a letter that threatens our livelihood. Or maybe when wounds from the past keep getting triggered, keeping us in a state of stress.

These are times we realize God is all we have. He is the only One who can save us. He is who will rescue us. These desperate seasons require God's intervention to deliver us from strangling stress into perfect peace. And when we call out to Him, scripture reminds us He will get us out of those tight spots. Friend, ask God for freedom from anxious fear. He is your hope!

## *Pray:*

*God, I know I have a part to play, but thank You for being willing to meet me more than halfway. I get so overwhelmed by stress that I often shut down. It paralyzes me. I realize I need to be more honest with You about my fears and worries because You are the One who will save me. I'm asking for Your help now. In Jesus' name I pray. Amen.*

# HUMAN NATURE VERSUS THE SPIRIT'S LEADING

———— Read Romans 8:1–17 ————

### Key Verse:

*Those who live as their human nature tells them to, have their minds controlled by what human nature wants. Those who live as the Spirit tells them to, have their minds controlled by what the Spirit wants. To be controlled by human nature results in death; to be controlled by the Spirit results in life and peace.*

ROMANS 8:5–6 GNT

### Understand:

- If you were to be honest, would you say you follow human nature or God's will more often? What needs to change?

- What might be the benefits of letting the Holy Spirit lead in your life? What keeps you from it?

*Apply*:

There is a natural tension as we try to walk out our faith in the real world. It's a battle between our human nature and what God wants for us. It's deciding if we're going to satisfy our fleshly desires or follow the Holy Spirit's leading. And it's this tension that fuels stress, especially when we know what we're doing isn't His will for us.

The path of faith isn't always easy because it challenges you to make hard choices. You're asked to surrender negative habits for godly ones. It's a call to let the Lord override your thoughts with His and to follow His ways over yours. And when you do, you'll soon discover that peace replaces the stress. God's way may be difficult at times, but there's no doubt the payoff is well worth it.

*Pray*:

*God, I know my human nature is strong. I have very real desires for my life that are hard to give up. At the same time, I want to be a woman full of faith. Help me surrender my will to Yours. Fill my head with Your thoughts over my fleshly ones. I want my life to be pleasing to You in every way, and I need Your help to make that happen. In Jesus' name I pray. Amen.*

# KEEPING PERFECT PEACE

—————— Read Isaiah 26:1–21 ——————

*Key Verse:*

*You will keep the peace, a perfect peace, for all who trust in You, for those who dedicate their hearts and minds to You. So trust in the Eternal One forever, for He is like a great Rock— strong, stable, trustworthy, and lasting.*
ISAIAH 26:3–4 VOICE

*Understand:*

- Recall a situation in which trusting God produced peace in your heart. What was significant about that time?

- What is the difference between God's peace and the kind of peace the world offers?

## *Apply:*

When life comes crashing down around you, trust God. When the call comes, the husband walks out, the betrayal is revealed, or the insecurity gets tangled, cry to the Lord with all your might. He is the One who brings hope in those hopeless moments. He is how you find the strength over stress to carry on. God is why you can have a clear mind to process the situation.

Starting today, choose to dedicate your heart and mind to the Lord. How do you walk that out? Invite God into your day and talk to Him about the circumstances causing fear, worry, and stress. Ask Him to speak into those situations and listen for His voice. Meditate on key scriptures that both challenge and encourage you. Be quick to remind yourself of His promises to save those He loves when they cry out. And grab onto His peace every day so nothing can take it away.

## *Pray:*

*God, I don't have much peace. Instead, I feel constantly stirred up with stress and sadness. I am easily tripped up by the words and actions of others. But I know peace is possible when I dedicate my heart and mind to You. Please be a strong and stable force in my life, trustworthy in all things. I need You. In Jesus' name I pray. Amen.*

# THE STRESS OF RELATIONSHIPS

———— Read Jeremiah 17:1–27 ————

## Key Verse:

*But blessed is the man who trusts in the Lord and has made the Lord his hope and confidence. He is like a tree planted along a riverbank, with its roots reaching deep into the water—a tree not bothered by the heat nor worried by long months of drought. Its leaves stay green, and it goes right on producing all its luscious fruit.*

JEREMIAH 17:7–8 TLB

## Understand:

- How do you think trusting God blesses your relationships?

- Today's verse paints a powerful image of a tree. What is the Holy Spirit saying to you through it?

## Apply:

Relationships are a huge source of stress because we can't control the other person—at least not for long. We may be in a rough patch where we're fighting all the time. We may feel disconnected and worried. And we may obsess over fixing the relationship, feeling the stress of it every day. But until we take a step back and trust the Lord to make straight the crooked path, our heart will remain heavy.

Friend, take your worry to God. Talk to Him about your anxious thoughts. When you trust the Lord with those you care about, you'll find an amazing sense of peace and a greater perspective on the situation. Those deep roots of faith will hold you steady and nourish you with His goodness. Trusting will gently rekindle your confidence. And over time, your anxiousness will diminish as your hope of relational restoration grows.

## Pray:

*God, I'm struggling in some key relationships right now, and it's causing so much stress. I've tried to fix things myself, but it's only deepened my anxiety because I can't control the situation. I'm waving the white flag in defeat. I give up. I'm surrendering my worry and trusting You'll make everything right. I'm placing my confidence in You! In Jesus' name I pray. Amen.*

# GOD'S SUPERNATURAL ABILITIES

---- Read Psalm 46:1–11 ----

## Key Verse:

*Surrender your anxiety. Be still and realize that I am God. I am God above all the nations, and I am exalted throughout the whole earth. Here he stands! The Commander! The mighty Lord of Angel Armies is on our side! The God of Jacob fights for us!*

PSALM 46:10–11 TPT

## Understand:

- Where are you striving to fix things you're not called to fix? Where are you acting like God?

- Write down what today's verse says about who God is. Which description means the most to you right now?

## *Apply*:

For many, anxiety looks ugly on us. We cry a lot. Complain a lot. Exhaust our friends and family by rehashing every situation ad nauseam. We mope around, throwing pity party after pity party. And while we should be trusting God with all we have, we don't. Instead, we milk it for all it's worth, keeping stress alive and thriving.

Today's passage of scripture is important. When God tells you to be silent, listen. When He tells you to know He is God and nothing you can do will get you that title, obey. Taking these two commands seriously is key to successfully surrendering your anxiety. Let the Lord in all His power and magnificence work His supernatural abilities in your stressful situation. He can fix it. You cannot.

## *Pray*:

*God, I confess that I sometimes take on Your role in my situations. Forgive me for thinking I am capable of the amazing things only You can do. Today's scripture was a powerful reminder that You are God and I am not. Knowing that, I surrender my anxiety and trust You to bring healing and restoration. I will be silent and still as I wait on Your intervention. I love You, and I trust You. In Jesus' name I pray. Amen.*

# TRUSTING IN THE WAITING

—————— **Read Isaiah 40:1–31** ——————

*Key Verse:*

*But those who trust in the LORD for help will find their strength renewed. They will rise on wings like eagles; they will run and not get weary; they will walk and not grow weak.*
ISAIAH 40:31 GNT

*Understand:*

- Where are you struggling to trust God right now? What makes it difficult?

- Consider the relationship between trusting God and finding internal strength for the battle. What new revelation did you find?

- How can you walk this out in real time?

*Apply:*

When we're feeling stressed, waiting for relief or resolution is a tall order. We want immediate closure because we want the persistent ache in our chest to go away. And when it doesn't, we feel weaker and weaker as our strength to manage it all wanes. Our resolve melts. And we wave the white flag of surrender because all hope is gone, and we have nothing left to give.

But you have a choice. This is where your faith comes into play. Without fail, when you choose to trust the Lord in your mess your stress will lessen until it's gone. Your worry and fear will begin to dissipate. Anxious thoughts will start to slow. And when you trust Him in the waiting, your strength will renew, giving you the ability to navigate even the toughest of situations. Remember that your humanity will hit limitations, which is why your level of peace relies on your willingness to activate your faith.

*Pray:*

*God, I confess it's hard to trust You when I am desperate for immediate relief. I know You're not a genie in a bottle that grants every wish, so forgive me for the times I've treated You as such. I am choosing from today forward to be patient as I wait for You to intervene and renew my strength. I know You will never let me down. In Jesus' name I pray. Amen.*

# A CHEERFUL HEART OR
# A CRUSHED HEART?

―――――― Read Proverbs 17:1–28 ――――――

## Key Verse:

*A joyful, cheerful heart brings healing to both body
and soul. But the one whose heart is crushed
struggles with sickness and depression.*
PROVERBS 17:22 TPT

## Understand:

- Take inventory of how your heart is right now. Is it cheerful or crushed? Talk to God about it.

- Have you experienced the two heart conditions from today's verse? What role did faith play in them?

*Apply:*

Have you ever been in a tough season of life but still able to have joy? Can you recall a cheerfulness in your step when everything around you was a hot mess? If so, well done! That kind of response was a direct product of a relationship with the Lord. It's because you chose to trust God over everything else. And it was because you placed your faith in Him even though it took all you had.

If you've never experienced this, take courage! Your stress and fear don't have to pull you under. They don't have to crush your heart with heaps of hopelessness. But it takes intentionality. It's a deliberate choice to let your heart stay free from the stress of the day. And you can live this way when you choose faith over fear. It's possible when you know God is in control and has your best in mind.

*Pray:*

*God, I want the cheerful heart described in today's verse. I want to be able to choose this no matter what struggles I'm facing. Hard times won't stop, but I can decide how they affect me. And if I want a less stressed life, then I know the choice to make. You are a good Father who always has my back. Grow my faith so I never doubt that truth. In Jesus' name I pray. Amen.*

# THE GOD OF EVERYTHING

———— **Read Jeremiah 32:26–44** ————

*Key Verse:*

*Then GOD's Message came again to Jeremiah:
"Stay alert! I am GOD, the God of everything
living. Is there anything I can't do?*
JEREMIAH 32:26 MSG

*Understand:*

- Do you believe the messages in the Bible are for you too? Why or why not?

- Why is it important to stay alert, and how does this relate to stress and fear?

- If He is the God of everything, what part of your life does that not cover?

*Apply:*

If we truly believed God is the God of everything, how would we live differently? How would this truth affect our stress levels in parenting? How would it change how we felt when going through a tough season in marriage? If we knew this was true, what would our response be to financial failure, health scares, career crashes, and the like? What role would worry play in the ups and downs of life? These are good questions!

Let's choose to be women committed to trusting God no matter what. Let's greet every piece of bad news with steadfast faith. Let's turn our eyes to Jesus the moment life punches us in the gut. Let's be alert, watching for depression and discouragement to creep in. This powerful message may have come to Jeremiah, but it's for us too. Like him, let's recognize there's nothing God cannot do. He can fix it all, heal it all, restore it all, and open any door necessary.

*Pray:*

*God, forgive me for the times I've diminished Your magnificence in my mind. It's easy to believe You are all powerful until the stress hits, and then I grab for control. Mature my faith so I'm quick to remember You are the God of everything. There is nothing You cannot do! Help me believe it regardless of what I'm facing. Empower me to find peace and rest in You! In Jesus' name I pray. Amen.*

# WHEN THEY HAVE HURT YOU

———— Read Isaiah 41:1–20 ————

## Key Verse:

*"Do not yield to fear, for I am always near. Never turn your gaze from me, for I am your faithful God. I will infuse you with my strength and help you in every situation. I will hold you firmly with my victorious right hand. All who rage against you will be ashamed and disgraced. All who contend with you will perish and disappear."*
ISAIAH 41:10–11 TPT

## Understand:

- How does it make you feel to know that God is always near? What feeling does that evoke?

- What part of today's scripture connects to your heart the most? Why?

## Apply:

Fear and stress go hand in hand. We are stressed because we're scared about something, and we become more unsettled thanks to anxiety. It's a vicious cycle that keeps us stirred up. It may be fear about an upcoming job interview. A worrisome report from your child's school. Immoral images found on your husband's computer. Or hearing the hurtful gossip being spread about you.

Friend, in those moments remember today's passage of scripture. It's one that will steady your heart with precision. And it will remind you to keep your eyes on God rather than give in to the fear that feels so big. The stress may be pouring into your heart, but the Lord will instead infuse you with His strength. He will hold you firmly, and you will have peace. And He will be judge and jury to those who have hurt you.

## Pray:

*God, there is so much goodness in the Isaiah passage. You are near. You are faithful. You'll infuse with strength. You will help. I'll be held firmly. You will exact justice to my enemies. Thank You for loving me the way You do and for choosing to be involved in my life. Thank You for replacing fear and stress with Your peace! In Jesus' name I pray. Amen.*

# THE WEEDS OF WORRY

—— Read Matthew 13:1–23 ——

## Key Verse:

*"The seed cast in the weeds is the person who hears the kingdom news, but weeds of worry and illusions about getting more and wanting everything under the sun strangle what was heard, and nothing comes of it."*

MATTHEW 13:22 MSG

## Understand:

- How would you rate yourself on the worry scale? Are you a 1, not letting concern overtake you? Are you a 10, consumed day and night with fear? Or are you somewhere in between?

- What is the Holy Spirit saying to you right now?

- Based on today's devotional, how will you move forward?

## Apply:

Those pesky weeds of worry effectively choke out peace because they consume your thoughts. For example, when you're worried about your child or your marriage, it's hard to get anything done. It's all you think about. Worrying about anything in your life takes your mind off the things of God and keeps them on what's at hand. And the Word likens this to planting seeds of faith in unfertile places and expecting them to bloom. They simply won't.

But when you instead decide to embrace God's truth and promises, the weeds of worry will die off. Take every fear and anxious thought to the Lord and ask for help. Saturate yourself in the Word, knowing what He has to say about your situation. Water your faith in meditation, thinking on who God is and what He says He will do. And by doing so, you'll starve any and all apprehension from strangling your peace of mind.

## Pray:

*God, ouch. Today's message hit me hard and made me realize just how much I let worry choke my peace and joy. Honestly, I didn't even recognize all the places it's played out. Help me see it and be quick to take it to You for relief. I don't have to carry the burden of it any longer. In Jesus' name I pray. Amen.*

# LASHING OUT FROM STRESS

———————— Read Psalm 3:1–4:8 ————————

## Key Verse:

*Complain if you must, but don't lash out. Keep your mouth shut, and let your heart do the talking. Build your case before God and wait for his verdict.*

PSALM 4:4–5 MSG

## Understand:

- Has anyone lashed out at you in their stress? How did it feel? What was your response?

- How can you protect yourself from unloading on those you care about?

- What does it mean to let your heart do the talking?

## Apply:

Sometimes in our stress, we lash out at those we love. We tear into our kids for minor offenses. We are snarky and dismissive in response to our husband's innocuous comment. We point the finger of blame at a friend. And while it may offer temporary relief, stress comes right back. And even more, we've also hurt our friends and family. But where do we go when the stress and anxiety feel too big? Whom can we complain to and get it off our chest?

Let's remember that God is our safe place. We can tell Him anything without judgment. We can say how we feel without hurting anyone's feelings. We can let our stresses, fears, and worries out anytime and every time. Ask God for the wisdom to know when to unpack your feelings with those around you and when to talk only with Him. Sometimes keeping our mouth shut from spewing our anxiety is the kindest thing we can do.

## Pray:

*God, I confess the times I've been unkind in how I have treated those around me. Stress has caused me to say things better left unsaid. Help me be wise with my words. Help me know when to speak and when to stay silent. And let me always be prompted to unpack my fears and worries with You. I know You'll always listen. In Jesus' name I pray. Amen.*

# THE COMPANION OF FEAR

—————— Read Isaiah 35:1–10 ——————

## Key Verse:

*Tell those who worry, the anxious and fearful,
"Take strength; have courage! There's nothing
to fear. Look, here—your God! Right here is
your God! The balance is shifting; God will right
all wrongs. None other than God will give you
success. He is coming to make you safe."*
ISAIAH 35:4 VOICE

## Understand:

- Would those around you say you're full of worry
  and fear?

- How does the knowledge of God's presence help
  you shift the balance between fear and faith?

## Apply:

*There is nothing to fear.* Too often, those words do nothing to make us feel better because we don't believe them. Fear is a constant companion, and we experience it all day long. We are afraid the diagnosis will be devastating. We worry about the state of the world. We're stressed we won't be able to make the payment. We are terrified that argument may have been the last straw. For many of us, fear is very real.

God's presence has the power to calm our anxious heart. It has a supernatural effect that brings peace into chaotic situations. Knowing He is with us creates a sense of calm. We feel seen and safe. No one can explain how the Lord does it, but He does, and we are grateful. So when fear is stirred up and you're overwhelmed, take a deep breath and invite God in.

## Pray:

*God, fear is a big deal in my life. I'm realizing it is the lens I look at life through. The reality is that I'm afraid of both big things and little things. But I know Your presence will make all the difference. I am inviting You into my fear and waiting for Your supernatural peace to calm my stressed-out heart. In Jesus' name I pray. Amen.*

# DETERMINED AND CONFIDENT

―――― Read Deuteronomy 31:1–29 ――――

## Key Verse:

*"Be determined and confident. Do not be afraid
of them. Your God, the Lord himself, will be with
you. He will not fail you or abandon you."*
DEUTERONOMY 31:6 GNT

## Understand:

- Think about what fear has robbed from you. Ask God for His perspective and healing.

- What does it mean to you that God will not fail you?

- In your own words, describe how His presence brings goodness into your life.

## Apply:

One way to beat stress is to adopt an attitude of determination. It's finding the resolve to not let anything stop you from getting what you're after. It's digging deep for courage and willpower to override the fear. And it requires a tremendous amount of grit to move past the anxiety that tries to paralyze you. Without the Lord, you are destined for stress, struggles, and strife. Things feel hopeless, and you feel helpless. But with God, you can do it.

So go ahead, friend. Sign up for the class. Say yes to the promotion. Agree to take on the project. Be part of the movement. Decide to try it again. Open your heart up to a second chance. Choose to forgive anyway. Anxiety has been beaten. God will not fail you. He will not abandon you. Knowing that, thrive because with Him there's no room for fear and stress.

## Pray:

*God, give me strength to push stress aside and embrace the next right step forward. I need Your help to find determination and courage. I need willpower. And I'm asking for You to empower me to live with confidence. I don't want anything to keep me from living the life You've planned for me in advance, so bless me with divine boldness. In Jesus' name I pray. Amen.*

# LET GOD BE YOUR SAFE HOUSE

———— Read Psalm 9:1–20 ————

### Key Verse:

*God's a safe-house for the battered, a sanctuary during bad times. The moment you arrive, you relax; you're never sorry you knocked.*
PSALM 9:9–10 MSG

### Understand:

- If God is a safe house, what does that mean to you? How can this understanding help you manage stress and fear every day?

- Are you in a bad season of life right now? Talk to the Lord and share your heart. Tell Him what you need. He's listening.

## Apply:

When you feel picked on and battered in life, it creates a constant level of stress. Between feeling the pain from others and waiting for the next round of punches, you become hypervigilant. You put your guard up to try to shield yourself from more pain. Cynicism sets in. Pessimism develops. And you foster fear, doubt, and an anxious heart. These feeble attempts at self-protection are short lived and altogether unreliable.

Friend, grab onto God and let Him be your safe house. In this life, you will have difficulties until you see Jesus face-to-face. It's guaranteed. But when you take your weary and wounded heart to the Lord, you'll find sanctuary. He will speak truth into your spirit and encourage you with gentleness. He'll build you up with courage and confidence. And God will fill you with peace as He removes the power of stress and strife.

## Pray:

*God, this has been a rough season of life. I'm feeling beat up and beat down in so many ways. I know I've put up walls of self-protection, but they aren't effective. You're the only One who can fortify my heart for battle. Give me confidence and courage to stand up for myself so stress doesn't settle on me any longer. I cannot do this without You. In Jesus' name I pray. Amen.*

# WHY YOU CAN STAND STRONG

———— Read 2 Corinthians 4:1–18 ————

## *Key Verse:*

*Though we experience every kind of pressure, we're not crushed. At times we don't know what to do, but quitting is not an option. We are persecuted by others, but God has not forsaken us. We may be knocked down, but not out.*
2 CORINTHIANS 4:8–9 TPT

## *Understand:*

- Based on what you're facing in life, how does today's verse make you feel? What encouragement does it offer?

- Compare and contrast what Paul (author of today's verse) says we may face in life versus what our response in faith should be. What stands out?

## Apply:

Let today's verse be something to cling to when life tries to beat you up. Because the truth is life will throw plenty of curveballs. It may be doing so right now. But knowing that with God we can weather any storm should be the encouragement we need to not give up. Stress and fear are part of life, but if we ask God, He will make us strong enough to face it.

Your career may be in shambles. Your finances may be rock bottom. Your kids may be on the wrong path. Your health may be failing. Your marriage may be in deep trouble. And you may feel more alone than ever before. But you're not crushed. It may be a tough season, but quitting isn't an option. God hasn't forsaken you even though you're facing serious strife. Life may be knocking you down, but your faith will help you get back to your feet.

## Pray:

*God, I feel encouraged to stand strong when life deals me a terrible hand. Thank You for reminding me that when I activate my faith, I'm able to weather whatever comes my way. I am not a victim. I'm a victor. And be it stress or strife, I will be able to make it through. In Jesus' name I pray. Amen.*

# PEACE OF HEART

—————— Read Colossians 3:1–25 ——————

## Key Verse:

*Most of all, let love guide your life, for then
the whole church will stay together in perfect
harmony. Let the peace of heart that comes from
Christ be always present in your hearts and lives,
for this is your responsibility and privilege as
members of his body. And always be thankful.*
COLOSSIANS 3:14–15 TLB

## Understand:

- Think of all the ways you've tried to find peace in
  the past. Were they earthly solutions or were they
  God's way?

- What does it mean when today's verse says having
  peace of heart always present is "your responsibility and privilege as members of his body"?

## *Apply:*

It's fair to say we're all searching for that peace of heart where we're settled and feel safe from stress. And while short lived, chances are we've tried a million different ways to secure it. We've used food to calm us down. We've shopped till we've dropped. We've binged Netflix or lost ourselves in books that take us far away from this life. We've meditated or taken yoga classes. We've taken long walks outside. No doubt, we've been looking for earthly ways to calm our anxious heart.

But the beautiful truth is this peace of heart comes from Christ alone. Scripture tells us it's not only a privilege we receive as followers but also a responsibility to walk out. From peace flows a deeper ability to love. And loving those around you creates harmony in relationships. We're not the only ones to benefit from a less stressed life.

## *Pray:*

*God, I'm asking for Your peace to reign in my heart every day so I can live stress-free and be a blessing to others. I know it comes from You alone. There is no earthly substitute for it. In Jesus' name I pray. Amen.*

# AN INVITATION TO REST

—————— Read Matthew 11:1–30 ——————

*Key Verse:*

*"Are you tired? Worn out? Burned out on religion?
Come to me. Get away with me and you'll recover
your life. I'll show you how to take a real rest. Walk
with me and work with me—watch how I do it.
Learn the unforced rhythms of grace. I won't lay
anything heavy or ill-fitting on you. Keep company
with me and you'll learn to live freely and lightly."*
MATTHEW 11:28–30 MSG

*Understand:*

- Consider the state of your heart right now. What is
the overwhelming feeling? What is the Holy Spirit
asking of you?

- Reread today's verse and think about how walking
this out would change your current situation. How
will you respond?

## *Apply*:

God is inviting you to rest in Him. Doesn't that sound delightful? He is calling you to take a break from the stress and strife pulling you down and instead spend time in His presence. What will you find there? Grace. Peace. Restoration. Rejuvenation. The Lord says you'll learn to live in freedom. You will recover your life. You'll feel light again.

Friend, what feels heavy today? Are you feeling overwhelmed by your calendar? Are you trying to navigate too many strong personalities? Have you been running at this pace for too long? Is it becoming hard to keep your insecurities tucked away? Take God up on His offer. Choose to get away with Him, be it an hour or a day. Give yourself time to sit in His presence and let the Lord remove and replace. It will make all the difference.

## *Pray*:

*God, what a beautiful invitation. I am humbled You would call me into Your presence in such a beautiful way. Sometimes I feel unworthy. But Lord, today I am saying yes and asking for Your peace to bring my life into balance and into alignment with Your will. Thank You for caring. In Jesus' name I pray. Amen.*

# THE VALLEY OF
# DEEPEST DARKNESS

———————— Read Psalm 23:1–6 ————————

## *Key Verse*:

*Even when your path takes me through the valley
of deepest darkness, fear will never conquer me,
for you already have! Your authority is my strength
and my peace. The comfort of your love takes away
my fear. I'll never be lonely, for you are near.*

PSALM 23:4 TPT

## *Understand*:

- What valleys of darkness have you walked through
  lately? Where was God in it?

- Compare and contrast the difference between
  trusting the Lord in these dark seasons and choosing to walk them alone. What stands out the most?

## *Apply*:

For some, believing it may be God taking us through the valley of deepest darkness is confusing. Maybe we never considered He uses it for our benefit and His glory. But when He does, God stays with us through it all. Even more, when we trust Him, fear doesn't have to be part of the journey. We don't have to stress about how it will all turn out because God has already made a way.

If you lean on the Lord, you'll be invincible. You will have His strength and peace coursing through your veins. You'll feel comfort rather than fear. You'll feel loved, not alone. And no matter what you're facing, God will give you everything to rise victorious. Maybe that's why God's path sometimes leads us into the valley. It's a powerful example of who God is and what He can do. And when we understand it, this truth will revolutionize how we stand strong in stressful and scary situations.

## *Pray*:

*God, regardless of how I ended up here, I need to feel Your presence in the valley. Help me grab onto You for safety and sanity rather than anyone or anything else. You are my Deliverer! With You next to me, stress and fear have no power. I will be victorious! In Jesus' name I pray. Amen.*

# THE HASSLES OF DAILY LIFE

––––––––––– Read Luke 21:1–38 –––––––––––

## Key Verse:

*So be careful. Guard your hearts. They can be made
heavy with moral laxity, with drunkenness, with the
hassles of daily life. Then the day I've been telling
you about might catch you unaware and trap you.*

LUKE 21:34 VOICE

## Understand:

- What would it look like for you to guard your heart?
  What are you doing right? What are some steps
  you can take to be more vigilant?

- Think about what is making your heart heavy these
  days. What hassles feel overwhelming? Where is the
  heaviness of heart from? Talk to the Lord about them.

*Apply:*

Guarding our heart isn't a once and done process. It's an active choice we must make every day. There are countless situations that threaten us with stress and fear. Sometimes anxious thoughts bring a flood of uneasiness without warning. We can let our morality slide and quickly find ourselves in dangerous waters. And when we are reckless with our boundaries, the consequences are often heavy.

The Word of God is full of commands designed to keep the hassles of daily life at bay. They're there to help you be strong, especially when storms hit. When you're told to guard your heart, it's for a good reason because it keeps you from crumbling under the weight of worry. It keeps you focused on God's promises. And if your desire is to live a less stressed life, this is how you do it. Trust His commands and remember the Lord has your best in mind.

*Pray:*

*God, help me know the best ways to guard my heart. Give me eyes and ears to know when trouble is brewing. And let me remember that my effectiveness is rooted in my faith. You are why I can stand in victory. You're why I can live faithfully. In Jesus' name I pray. Amen.*

# HAPPINESS IN SUFFERING?

———— Read 1 Peter 3:1–22 ————

### Key Verse:

*But even if you should suffer for doing what
is right, how happy you are! Do not be
afraid of anyone, and do not worry.*
1 PETER 3:14 GNT

### Understand:

- Think about what suffering has looked like for you. How have you responded to it? Looking back, can you see God working in it?

- Journal about the times you chose the hard way because you knew it was the right way. What was the end result? How have those decisions helped you today?

## Apply:

Suffering is part of the human experience. No one gets out of life unscathed by its effects. There will be seasons of suffering because of the bad choices you've made. There will be times you'll suffer because of the bad choices others have made that directly affect you. And scripture is clear when it says you will also suffer for doing what is right. But friend, even when that's the case, you can find happiness.

So often the right thing is the hard thing. God smiles when you choose it anyway, especially knowing stress and fear are often by-products. When you stand up for the underdog, speak out hard truth, refuse to bow to dangerous groupthink, and take the road less traveled, the Lord is delighted. And when you feel His delight deep in your spirit, happiness and peace will radiate.

## Pray:

*God, I have suffered so much in my life, and it's been challenging to stay positive. But I now understand that it's Your delight in my right choices—even if they are the hardest ones to make—that will bring perspective so I can experience happiness in my suffering. I appreciate how Your economy works because it's so much better than anything this world has to offer. I love You! In Jesus' name I pray. Amen.*

# PLANNED IN ADVANCE

—————— Read Ephesians 2:1–22 ——————

## Key Verse:

*We have become his poetry, a re-created people that will fulfill the destiny he has given each of us, for we are joined to Jesus, the Anointed One. Even before we were born, God planned in advance our destiny and the good works we would do to fulfill it!*
EPHESIANS 2:10 TPT

## Understand:

- If you're worried about who you are and what your purpose is, talk to God. Be honest about your fears and insecurities and ask Him to solidify these truths in your heart.

- What is the Holy Spirit speaking to you regarding your destiny being planned in advance?

*Apply:*

Sometimes we get stressed out because we're struggling to know who we are—our identity. We wonder what we're here for. What is our purpose? And we worry that if we don't know our destiny, we won't be able to walk it out. Fear may set in as we're afraid of missing out. And so we walk around full of anxiety, unable to rest in the truth of who God created us to be. Not only is it exhausting, but it robs us of joy and peace.

Reread today's verse and let it sink in. It's important to understand God's truths about your identity. Friend, choose to believe—based solely in scripture—that you are an intentional creation with a specific destiny planned in advance. You were created with a purpose, and scripture says you will fulfill it through your words and actions because you are connected to Jesus.

*Pray:*

*God, I confess having fear and stress surrounding my identity and destiny. Both feel mysterious. In your kindness, would You open my heart to hear Your voice solidify these in me? Lead me to scripture that affirms Your truths. Speak into my confusion. I want to stand strong in who You created me to be. In Jesus' name I pray. Amen.*

# IT'S NOT ALL UP TO YOU

———— Read 2 Corinthians 3:1–18 ————

*Key Verse:*

*We carry this confidence in our hearts because
of our union with Christ before God. Yet we don't
see ourselves as capable enough to do anything
in our own strength, for our true competence
flows from God's empowering presence.*
2 CORINTHIANS 3:4-5 TPT

*Understand:*

- What kind of pressure do you place on yourself to handle things in your own strength? How might that be misguided?

- Realizing God is God and you are not, why do you expect yourself (or let others expect you) to be fully capable and competent?

## *Apply*:

Take a deep breath, friend. It's not all up to you. You don't have to figure it out on your own. Its success doesn't sit on your shoulders alone. You may have been told by others that it does. They may have put the weight of it on you to carry. But God fully understands the limitations you face because He created you. He knows where you need His intervention.

There is relief in recognizing you're unable to function without God's help. It's comforting to know you are not fully capable in your own strength. And there is peace in admitting that without the Lord's empowering presence in your life, you'll fall short every time. Your confidence comes from God. He is the One who makes up the difference and fills in the gaps. Don't stress because you can't handle things on your own. You weren't designed to.

## *Pray*:

*God, help me have realistic expectations of myself and let me keep the expectations others place on me to be realistic too. I am happy to embrace my limitations because doing so acknowledges how desperately I need You. I trust You to empower me in the right ways and at the right time to do Your work. In Jesus' name I pray. Amen.*

# HEART TROUBLE

—————— Read 1 John 3:1–24 ——————

## Key Verse:

*Whenever our hearts make us feel guilty and remind us of our failures, we know that God is much greater and more merciful than our conscience, and he knows everything there is to know about us. My delightfully loved friends, when our hearts don't condemn us, we have a bold freedom to speak face-to-face with God.*

1 JOHN 3:20–21 TPT

## Understand:

- Think about the difference between how you think and how God thinks based on today's scripture. What stands out the most?

- How does self-condemnation affect your ability and willingness to talk to God? Have you seen this in your own life?

*Apply:*

Our hearts are easily swayed into believing certain ways because of our circumstances. The hurtful things people say and how they treat us negatively affect what we think about ourselves. With little provocation, we easily subscribe to guilt and shame as we replay our failures over and over. Too often, we let our heart beat us up for feeling one way or another. The reality is the heart is full of emotions and feelings that stress us out and cause fear. And while what we feel matters greatly, most of the time it isn't factual.

But God sees right through a deceptive heart. He sees the full picture of who we are—the good and the not so good—and loves us anyway. Where we can't extend grace to ourselves, He can without fail. Where we obsess on shortcomings, God sees His beloved daughter. Ask God to remove self-condemnation so you can see yourself as He does.

*Pray:*

*God, the heart is so deceptive, and I have experienced self-condemnation because of it. Thank You for knowing me and seeing goodness. Remind me of that when I begin to beat myself up. And heal that tendency in me because I don't want anything to stifle my relationship with You. In Jesus' name I pray. Amen.*

# THE SOURCE OF HOPE

——————— **Read Romans 15:1–29** ———————

## *Key Verse:*

*I pray that God, the source of all hope, will infuse
your lives with an abundance of joy and peace
in the midst of your faith so that your hope will
overflow through the power of the Holy Spirit.*
ROMANS 15:13 VOICE

## *Understand:*

- In your opinion, what does it mean for God to
  infuse your life with an abundance of peace? How
  would that change your current situation?

- The Holy Spirit plays a role in hope. What is it?

- What role do you play in hope?

*Apply:*

Sometimes what we need more than anything is a good ol'-fashioned dose of hope. We need to feel like things will get better—that all will be okay in the end. We need to know the light at the end of the tunnel isn't a train barreling in our direction without brakes. And that true hope comes directly from the Lord. He is your Source. In the middle of your mess, God can drop it onto your heart and change everything in an instant.

Where are you desperate to exchange stress for hope? Are you walking through a long and painful divorce? Are your bills piling up faster than your income can keep up? Do you feel alone and abandoned? Did you just discover a betrayal? Are you craving friendships? Are you crushed with grief? Is your job coming to an end? Ask God to infuse your life with an abundance of joy and peace through His Holy Spirit. And then wait as He blesses you.

*Pray:*

*God, please infuse my life with hope right now.*
*At every turn, I'm getting bad news, and I am*
*overwhelmed with stress and fear. Activate Your Spirit*
*to let hope overflow in my life so I can testify to Your*
*goodness in tough places. In Jesus' name I pray. Amen.*

# THE STRESS OF
# SELF-CONFIDENCE

---------- Read Proverbs 28:1–28 ----------

## *Key Verse*:

*Self-confident know-it-alls will prove to be fools. But when you lean on the wisdom from above, you will have a way to escape the troubles of your own making.*
PROVERBS 28:26 TPT

## *Understand*:

- Would others in your life describe you as a self-confident know-it-all?

- Is it wrong to lean on your own wisdom? Why or why not?

- How would things be different if you leaned on God's knowledge over your own?

## Apply:

We get into trouble when we decide it's our way or the highway. When we think we know best above all others, it should be a red flag that we're in way over our head. And the stress creeps in when our way fails. We feel it when others won't listen to us or follow our lead. In the end, we're angry and humiliated and full of anxiety. And even more, the Bible says we are fools. Ouch.

So what's the solution? It's realizing our wisdom and discernment are flawed, just like everyone else's. It's replacing the know-it-all attitude with the One who really does know it all. It's leaning on the Lord for all answers, trusting Him for redirection. It's following His lead rather than demanding your own way. It's being open to what other faith-filled followers bring to the table. And if you want to live a less stressed life, being humble and activating your faith are good starts.

## Pray:

*God, forgive me for the times I've thought of myself as above others—above You. I believe You created me to be a capable woman, but I get into trouble when I forget to be humble. Help me see the good ideas and suggestions in others as well as firmly seek Your wisdom in all things. In Jesus' name I pray. Amen.*

# HOW TO GUARANTEE STRESS

———————— Read Psalm 20:1–9 ————————

### *Key Verse:*

*See those people polishing their chariots,
and those others grooming their horses? But
we're making garlands for GOD our God. The
chariots will rust, those horses pull up lame—
and we'll be on our feet, standing tall.*

PSALM 20:7–8 MSG

### *Understand:*

- Why do you think it's easier to trust things of the
  world over God?

- In the past, what have you leaned on for help when
  stressed out? What changes will you make today?

*Apply:*

If you place your faith in anything other than God, stress will be an everyday part of your life. It will be a staple. Stress and fear will be constant companions that stick close. You may find earthly options that offer temporary relief, but they won't help in the long run, and soon you'll be filled with anxious thoughts once again. The Word is clear that everything here will fade away. But not God.

When you need help and hope, He is the only safe place. If you think about it, God has never let you down. He has a perfect track record in your life. He may not follow your timeline because His is perfect. He may not respond in the way you want because God knows what's best. Having faith means choosing to believe God's heart for you is always good and His plans for you always perfect. But if you'll let Him be the One you run to when life gets hard, you will find peace and comfort regardless of your messy circumstances.

*Pray:*

*God, I confess all the times I've trusted in earthly solutions for my stress. I have put my faith in things other than You. Forgive me, Lord. From today forward, please help me be quick to put my faith in You over anything else. Give me an extra measure of belief. In Jesus' name I pray. Amen.*

# TOMORROW IS IN GOD'S HANDS

————— Read James 4:1–17 —————

## Key Verse:

*But you don't have a clue what tomorrow may bring. For your fleeting life is but a warm breath of air that is visible in the cold only for a moment and then vanishes! Instead you should say, "Our tomorrows are in the Lord's hands and if he is willing we will live life to its fullest and do this or that."*
JAMES 4:14–15 TPT

## Understand:

- Take inventory of the stress you're experiencing right now. Are they things of today or tomorrow?

- If you truly believed every tomorrow is in God's hands, how would you live differently?

*Apply:*

Stay in today, friend. There's enough fear and stress in the here and now to manage without heaping the worries of tomorrow on as well. The temptation we face is to look ahead. The problem is that when we do, we rarely predict good things. More often than not, we decide we're facing horrible outcomes and endings, so the stress associated with that piles on and pulls us underwater.

Reread James's suggestion because it's so important. Find peace in knowing your tomorrow is in God's hands. He has complete knowledge of everything good or bad that may or will happen. Even more, He is already working in it. That means you don't have to worry. You don't have to live stressed out. Why? Because the Lord has a full understanding of what the future brings, and He will make a way. When you trust Him, you will see the path.

*Pray:*

*God, too often my tomorrows get ahead of me.*
*They taunt me and cause fear and anxiety because*
*I can't control them. Help me rest in You and trust*
*You're already working things out for my benefit and*
*Your glory. I don't have to stress because I know You*
*have me. Thank You. In Jesus' name I pray. Amen.*

# SIMPLY ENDURE

— Read Hebrews 10:1–36 —

## *Key Verse*:

*Remember this, and do not abandon your
confidence, which will lead to rich rewards.
Simply endure, for when you have done as God
requires of you, you will receive the promise.*
HEBREWS 10:35–36 VOICE

## *Understand*:

- Knowing that enduring and obeying God brings
  blessing, where are you encouraged to stand strong?

- Where have you seen this concept play out in your
  life? Have you seen it in the lives of others? How
  does it encourage you today?

## *Apply:*

Even when it's hard, endure. Even when others criticize or judge you, continue doing what God has asked. When you want to give up, dig deep for perseverance. Ask the Lord to give you strength to stand strong. Nothing of great value is easy to do, so choose to stay the course. Why? Because the Word of God says that when we have done what He has asked, there will be a blessing on the other side.

In those times, ask the Lord for comfort to combat the stress. Ask for peace to override fear. He will give you exactly what you need to prevail. God will provide the wisdom for good choices, the steadfastness to keep going, the joy to bear the process, the confidence to take the next step, and the courage to overcome obstacles. Friend, you will always want what's on the other side of obedience. Simply endure.

## *Pray:*

*God, it's easy to read the words in today's*
*devotional, but walking them out is much harder.*
*I'm asking You to help me simply endure because*
*I know there is a rich reward on the other side.*
*I trust You to give me what I need to obey Your*
*commands. And I am so grateful You understand*
*the struggle and are willing to fill in the gaps of our*
*human condition. In Jesus' name I pray. Amen.*

# OVERCOMING FEAR

---------- Read Psalm 27:1-14 ----------

## Key Verse:

*The Lord is my light and my salvation; he protects me*
*from danger—whom shall I fear? When evil men come*
*to destroy me, they will stumble and fall! Yes, though*
*a mighty army marches against me, my heart shall*
*know no fear! I am confident that God will save me.*
PSALM 27:1-3 TLB

## Understand:

- Whom or what do you fear? What would it look like
  for you to choose to trust God instead?

- Rewrite today's verse and make it your own. Add
  your details, and let it be an encouragement that
  God is willing and able to intervene!

## Apply:

Fear is a big deal because it becomes the lens we look at life through. We use it to determine what our next move will be. We allow it to overwhelm us into shutting down emotionally. We let it validate our decision to hide from community. We let it overpower us until we become ineffective. And rather than live in victory and joy, we cower. Friend, if you're living this way right now, let it be a red flag.

The psalmist figured it out. He knew the power that came from trusting God more than anything else. He understood the weight of stress in life and the fear it created, but he didn't give in. He knew that when the worst situation was at hand, it was no match for God. Instead of giving in, he stood in faith and believed in the Lord's power to keep him safe and give him hope. What an amazing testimony that can strengthen us today!

## Pray:

*God, sometimes I forget You are bigger than my fears. I forget You're stronger than my stressors. Build in me confidence to believe in You no matter what. And grow my confidence to be fearless in every situation. In Jesus' name I pray. Amen.*

# SOWING AND REAPING THE GOOD STUFF

—————— Read Galatians 6:1–18 ——————

## *Key Verse:*

*Don't be misled: No one makes a fool of God. What a person plants, he will harvest. The person who plants selfishness, ignoring the needs of others—ignoring God!—harvests a crop of weeds. All he'll have to show for his life is weeds! But the one who plants in response to God, letting God's Spirit do the growth work in him, harvests a crop of real life, eternal life.*

GALATIANS 6:7–8 MSG

## *Understand:*

- Take inventory of the seeds you are sowing in your life. Write them down and decide whether they stay or go.

- Ask the Lord what crops He has planned for you. Are you on the same page? If not, what needs to change so you're following God's plan?

## Apply:

One of the most powerful concepts in the Bible is the relationship between sowing and reaping. The idea is that whatever you plant and promote is what you end up with in life. If you plant faith, it will grow. If you plant seeds of kindness, they will blossom in beautiful ways. But in the same vein, if you sow seeds of stress, the crop will produce more of the same.

This is why it's important to let God's Holy Spirit lead you. Let Him be the One to grow and mature the right crops in your life, because doing so guarantees it will be filled with the worthy things. The Lord's plan is to cultivate faith in you. He intends to produce crops like peace, joy, strength, and wisdom. So when the weeds of stress and fear spring up and threaten the good stuff, let God prune with purpose so nothing of value is choked out.

## Pray:

*God, help me sow the right seeds into my life. I want to be more intentional to follow Your lead so I'm working with You and not against You. In Jesus' name I pray. Amen.*

# THE STRESS OF STRIVING FOR RICHES

—————— Read Proverbs 23:1–35 ——————

## Key Verse:

*Don't wear yourself out trying to get rich;
restrain yourself! Riches disappear in the
blink of an eye; wealth sprouts wings and
flies off into the wild blue yonder.*
PROVERBS 23:4–5 MSG

## Understand:

- Do you have a healthy relationship with money? Would your closest friends and family agree?

- Where do you need to restrain yourself from striving for riches? What is the Holy Spirit saying to you right now?

*Apply:*

Wanting to live your best life is noteworthy. There is nothing wrong with wanting the fullness it offers. Trying to embrace life with gusto is wonderful, and the Lord wants you to enjoy the good things about it. But we get into trouble when we're striving for more for all the wrong reasons. And too often, we wear ourselves out from the desire to get rich, and it sets us up for stress.

Ask God for the gift of contentment. It helps us understand what we have is enough. It keeps up from being envious of others or spending more than we should just to keep up. It gives us perspective to understand what matters the most in life. And it allows us to live with peace over stress. The next time you feel anxiety from the pursuit of money, take it right to God and let Him remind you of what is true and right.

*Pray:*

*God, I'm convicted by today's devotional and scripture. I can see how my pursuit of riches has taken me out of Your plan and into loads of unwanted stress. Help me remember that what I have is enough and to enjoy the gifts I've been given rather than strive for more. I want to live with contentment, knowing You're all I need. In Jesus' name I pray. Amen.*

# WRITTEN ON HIS HAND

────────── Read Isaiah 49:1–26 ──────────

## *Key Verse:*

*Is it possible for a mother, however disappointed,
however hurt, to forget her nursing child? Can she
feel nothing for the baby she carried and birthed?
Even if she could, I, God, will never forget you.
Look here. I have made you a part of Me, written
you on the palms of My hands. Your city walls
are always on My mind, always My concern.*
ISAIAH 49:15–16 VOICE

## *Understand:*

- How can you relate to today's verse that talks
  about the relationship between mother and child?
  What does that awake in you?

- Have you felt the stress of abandonment? Journal
  about it.

- What is your reaction to knowing Your name is
  written on God's hand? How does that heal your
  heart?

*Apply:*

Few things sting more than being abandoned. To be pushed away and rejected by those you thought cared the most wounds deeply. But for most (if not all) of us, we're too familiar with this feeling. Have you experienced it? In the end, we're left feeling like throwaways. We feel unloved and unworthy. And the stress of not belonging sometimes feels like too much.

Let today's passage of scripture wash over your broken heart. It's a bold declaration by God that can bring healing to the wound of abandonment. Friend, He has written your name on the palm of His holy hand. Your name. Recognize how that deliberate act literally made you a part of Him. There is no better sense of belonging than being known by God in such a permanent way. So take a step back from stress and see the value He has spoken into your heart. People may walk away, but God never will.

*Pray:*

*God, You always make a way to restore my heart. You always know exactly what I need to hear, and Your timing is perfect. What a relief to know my name is on Your hand permanently and that You'll never abandon me. Thank You! In Jesus' name I pray. Amen.*

# HIS WRAPAROUND PRESENCE

─────── Read Psalm 62:1–12 ───────

## Key Verse:

*God's glory is all around me! His wraparound presence is all I need, for the Lord is my Savior, my hero, and my life-giving strength. Trust only in God every moment! Tell him all your troubles and pour out your heart-longings to him. Believe me when I tell you—he will help you!*

PSALM 62:7–8 TPT

## Understand:

- What does God's wraparound presence mean to you?

- In those seasons where you feel alone, how will today's scripture give you encouragement?

## Apply:

In those moments where you feel all alone, remember that His presence literally wraps around You. Just like your favorite oversized blanket, God's love will cover every inch of you from head to toe. Can you get an image of that in your mind? Friend, you're never alone because He is with you always. You cannot run from Him. You cannot hide. In God's infinite love, He never lets you out of His sight.

So when your husband walks away or your teenagers don't have time for you, feel the Lord's embrace. When your friends are sparce and you're not connecting well with coworkers, remember His wraparound presence. When stress and fear begin to speak lies about your worth as a single woman, sit with God and share your tears with Him. The truth of the matter is there's nothing that can separate you from your Father. His glory surrounds you always. And He is the One who will restore your heart and rejuvenate your spirit.

## Pray:

*God, let me feel Your presence in my life right now. I am not only alone but overwhelmed by a strong sense of loneliness. I know spending time with You will remind me I belong and am loved. Please meet me in this moment and encourage my weary and anxious heart. In Jesus' name I pray. Amen.*

# NEVER ENOUGH

--------- Read Psalm 33:1–22 ---------

## Key Verse:

*Even if a king had the best-equipped army, it would never be enough to save him. Even if the best warrior went to battle, he could not be saved simply by his strength alone. Human strength and the weapons of man are false hopes for victory; they may seem mighty, but they will always disappoint.*

PSALM 33:16–17 TPT

## Understand:

- What are the skills and abilities the Lord created in you? Write them down and take a moment to thank God for them.

- Do you believe He made you to be the savior for yourself or anyone else? Find scripture to back up your answer.

## Apply:

Make no mistake, your human effort needs divine reinforcement. You simply don't have the ability to fix and restore like God does. That's not to say you're incapable. When the Lord made you, He baked well-planned talents into your being. There is so much you're able to do with great passion and purpose. You have skills and life experiences that make you a well-rounded and powerful woman. But you don't have the strength to save. That rests with God alone.

Stress comes into play when you feel like your best isn't enough. When you try and fail at something important, your insecurities get triggered, your pride gets dinged, and stress most often follows. But what if you were never meant to be a savior for yourself or others? The truth is that position has already been filled by Jesus. Ask the Lord to change your thoughts so you don't assume the fix is up to you.

## Pray:

*God, forgive me for trying to step into Your shoes as the savior. So often, it happens without intentionality. I don't mean to take Your place, so forgive me. Give me unshakable confidence in You to know You're the only One who can save. And let me find peace in that beautiful truth. In Jesus' name I pray. Amen.*

# OWNING UP

---------- Read James 5:1–20 ----------

## *Key Verse:*

*So own up to your sins to one another and pray for one
another. In the end, you may be healed. Your prayers
are powerful when they are rooted in a righteous life.*
JAMES 5:16 VOICE

## *Understand:*

- Think about what a difference it would make in your
  own relationships to admit your fault, ask for forgiveness, and pray for the spirit of reconciliation.

- Why does the Enemy love broken relationships?

*Apply:*

When your relationship with someone is strained, find the courage to go to them and talk about it. It may be uncomfortable and stressful to think about, but something powerful happens when you're able to admit wrongdoing and extend forgiveness to one another. This next step will bring healing and hope as you choose to fight for your relationship.

The Enemy would like nothing more than to disrupt your marriage or friendships. He understands how fulfilling they can be. He knows how they bring encouragement and a sense of belonging. And if he can convince you to keep an offense against one another alive in your heart, then you lose out on the benefits of community. Don't allow stress or fear or hurt feelings to keep you closed off. Instead, ask the Lord for the courage and confidence to be the bigger person and address the situation. Ask Him to heal what's broken.

*Pray:*

*God, I've been so stressed out because of broken relationships. And while I know I have a part to play in them, my pride has kept me from admitting fault. Forgive me for caring more about being right than being righteous. Help me find the grit to own up to my sin and extend grace. I want healing between us. And I am resolved to make it happen. In Jesus' name I pray. Amen.*

# THE POWER OF GOD'S WORD

—————— Read Hebrew 4:1–16 ——————

*Key Verse:*

*The word of God is alive and active, sharper than any double-edged sword. It cuts all the way through, to where soul and spirit meet, to where joints and marrow come together. It judges the desires and thoughts of the heart.*
HEBREW 4:12 GNT

*Understand:*

- In your opinion, what does it mean to say God's Word is alive and active?

- Think of a time when a certain passage of scripture spoke directly to your heart. What was unique about it? What stood out?

## *Apply:*

God's Word is alive! It is active. And it slices through any fog or confusion you may be facing. That means what was written in its pages thousands of years ago is still valid today. Every promise documented in it is also for you. The Bible is still your best reference for righteous living and is time tested through and through. It's how God reveals Himself to those who seek Him. So rather than stress or worry about if your choices are right, open the Word and look for yourself.

Am I loving well? Is forgiveness an option? Can I lose my salvation? Does God condemn? Is peace possible? Am I alone? Will fear ever go away? How can I best manage stress? The answers to these questions are found in its pages—those and countless others. The Bible will challenge you, encourage you, bless you, and help you find the best ways to live a faith-filled life.

## *Pray:*

*God, thank You for Your Word. It's a gift full of mystery and intrigue. It both affirms and encourages. It instructs and convicts. Let it be a daily resource for me as I try to live my best life and get to know You better. In Jesus' name I pray. Amen.*

# IT'S OKAY TO MESS UP

──────── Read Philippians 1:1–30 ────────

### Key Verse:

*I am confident that the Creator, who has begun such a great work among you, will not stop in mid-design but will keep perfecting you until the day Jesus the Anointed, our Liberating King, returns to redeem the world.*
PHILIPPIANS 1:6 VOICE

### Understand:

- How does it feel to know God will never give up on you? Is that affirming? Annoying? Something else?

- Talk to God about any stress that may stem from worrying His love and acceptance of you is performance based.

## *Apply:*

Don't be discouraged when you mess up. Be careful to keep stress at bay when you fall short of your goal. You're not perfect, even when you work hard and focus. You will make mistakes. You will make unhealthy choices. You'll scream at the kids. You'll make snarky comments to your husband. You'll disappoint your boss. And you will hurt your friend's feelings. But that doesn't mean God is done with you.

What a blessing to know we get do-overs with Him. The Word is crystal clear when it says we are a work in progress. As a matter of fact, God will continue perfecting us until we see Him face-to-face. And even when we blow it, He won't give up. He won't stop mid-design, throw His hands in the air, and decide we're too far gone. God is patient and purposeful, so we don't ever have to be anxious that we've pushed Him too far.

## *Pray:*

*God, sometimes I worry that You may walk out on me too. I know I can be rebellious and selfish, so it's such a blessing to know I can't sin myself out of a relationship with You. I want to live in ways that are pleasing, but I can't do it alone. Mold me. Grow me. Make me into the woman You intended from the start. In Jesus' name I pray. Amen.*

# BE A PEACEMAKER

—————— Read Matthew 5:1–12 ——————

*Key Verse*:

*"You're blessed when you can show people
how to cooperate instead of compete or
fight. That's when you discover who you
really are, and your place in God's family."*
MATTHEW 5:9 MSG

*Understand*:

- What is God speaking to you about being a peace-maker or peacekeeper?

- Are there situations where He may be wanting to use you in this capacity? How does that make you feel?

## *Apply:*

Be a peacemaker. Be the kind of mom who teaches her kids to get along. Be the wife who advises her husband to connect better with coworkers. Be the friend who advises forgiveness and reconciliation. Be the advocate who offers compelling reasons to lay down offenses. The truth is that this world offers plenty of opportunities to compete and fight. We can easily justify our anger and frustration. But God says that when you show others how to cooperate instead—even if there is tension and hurt feelings—you will be blessed.

Think about how the state of the world would improve if we were able to listen to one another. We all need a way to de-stress and lessen levels of anxiety. If we decided different opinions weren't deal breakers, imagine how we could get along. Wouldn't it be delightful to have a spirited conversation with opposing ideas and not pick up offenses? Ask God to enable you to be a peacemaker!

## *Pray:*

*God, open my eyes and ears to see places where I can help bring peace. There is so much anger and offense in the world today, and the idea of being an agent of peace feels needed. If that is Your desire for me, I'll need help! It's intimidating to think I could work for You in that capacity, but I'm up for the challenge! In Jesus' name I pray. Amen.*

# WHAT'S YOUR MOTIVATION?

———————— Read Romans 8:1–27 ————————

## Key Verse:

*Those who are motivated by the flesh only pursue what benefits themselves. But those who live by the impulses of the Holy Spirit are motivated to pursue spiritual realities. For the sense and reason of the flesh is death, but the mind-set controlled by the Spirit finds life and peace.*
ROMANS 8:5–6 TPT

## Understand:

- Compare and contrast the differences between being motivated by the flesh and being motivated by the Spirit. What is most notable to you?

- What are some practical ways you can set your mind on God above yourself?

*Apply*:

Every day, we have a choice to make. We can either be motivated by what our flesh wants, or we can choose to listen to the Holy Spirit in us and follow His leading. One is purely focused on ourselves, our needs, and our desires. The other is setting those aside and pursuing the life God has planned for us. And it shouldn't surprise you that one opens the door to stress and the other settles our heart in peace. What will you choose?

It takes faith and help from God Himself to walk out a Christian life because it goes against our sinful nature and what society promotes. Choosing to have a mind controlled by the Spirit takes intentional surrendering of what we think is best. It's sacrificing what we want. And while many may see this as ridiculous and unnecessary, this kind of purposeful living brings peace in abundance. It keeps stress and fear at bay. And it delights God.

*Pray*:

*God, I understand the choices I have to make every day regarding how I live. I see the difference between Your way and mine. I know the results each will bring. But sometimes I still choose me. Forgive those choices and help me keep an eternal perspective so I can live a faith-filled life full of peace rather than stress. In Jesus' name I pray. Amen.*

# RIGHTEOUSNESS TRANSFERRED

———— **Read Romans 5:1–21** ————

### Key Verse:

*Our faith in Jesus transfers God's righteousness to us and he now declares us flawless in his eyes. This means we can now enjoy true and lasting peace with God, all because of what our Lord Jesus, the Anointed One, has done for us.*

ROMAN 5:1 TPT

### Understand:

- Think about what it means to be declared flawless in God's eyes. Tell Him what that means to you.

- Peace and stress are opposites. What does Jesus have to do with these? What changes because of Him?

## Apply:

Because of Jesus, you have been declared flawless in God's eyes. For some, this is hard to believe and embrace because of the life they have lived. They look at their seasons of sinning and decide this promise isn't for them. They're afraid and anxious about approaching the Lord, so they stay distant and discouraged. Don't let this be you. Don't let this kind of thinking keep you from living a faith-filled life. Don't let this block your enjoyment of His promised peace.

What Jesus did on the cross was extraordinary, and it had supernatural results that are available to you. His death paid the penalty of your sin once and for all. And if you believe Jesus to be the Son of God and your Savior, His righteousness has been transferred to you. From that point forward, you are His child and can enjoy peace with God. Stress and fear no longer have to rule. You are blessed!

## Pray:

*God, thank You for what Jesus did on the cross for me. Thank You that His sacrifice—Your sacrifice—has completely changed my life. To think I am declared flawless is amazing, especially knowing how very imperfect I am. I receive Your gift of salvation and the transfer of righteousness with humility and thanksgiving! In Jesus' name I pray. Amen.*

# HOW TO BE HAPPY

———————— Read Psalm 119:1–48 ————————

## Key Verse:

*Happy are the people who walk with integrity,
who live according to the teachings of the
Eternal. Happy are the people who keep His
decrees, who pursue Him wholeheartedly.*

PSALM 119:1–2 VOICE

## Understand:

• What is the connection between happiness and following God's commands? Do you see this in your own life?

• In your opinion, what does it mean to pursue God wholeheartedly? What changes might you need to make?

## *Apply*:

If you want to stay status quo—weighed down by worry and stress and fear—then your path is easy. Stay distant from God. Don't spend your time reading scripture or praying. Don't open up your heart to Him, unpacking your feelings. Live the way that feels best regardless of what God asks of you, and don't let integrity or truthfulness bog you down.

But if you want to be happy, an important step is choosing to embrace God's way of living. It's making the right, faithful decisions even though they aren't always the easiest. It means you spend time reading God's Word so you know His will for your life. It's setting aside time each day to spend in community with the Lord, talking to Him about your struggles and listening for His still, small voice to guide you. This is intentional living that will bless you tenfold.

## *Pray*:

*God, I want to be part of the happy people in the world—the ones whose faith is anchored in You. I want to embrace and live out your prescription for a faithful life. I want to care about Your commands and follow them every day. And I want to pursue a deeper relationship with You so my life points others to Your goodness. Give me the strength and wisdom to make this a reality. In Jesus' name I pray. Amen.*

# THE PROBLEM
# WITH BOASTING

—————— Read James 3:1–18 ——————

## Key Verse:

*But if there is bitter jealousy or competition
hiding in your heart, then don't deny it and try
to compensate for it by boasting and being phony.
For that has nothing to do with God's heavenly
wisdom but can best be described as the wisdom
of this world, both selfish and devilish.*

JAMES 3:14–15 TPT

## Understand:

- Take a moment to explore your heart, looking for places where there is jealousy or competition with others. Journal about it.

- Why is boasting dangerous? How can it backfire on you?

- What about you makes you proud? Tell God about it.

## *Apply*:

Boasting will always get us in trouble. The truth is there is no good reason we need to toot our own horn. Most of the time we boast because we want to be noticed. We want credit for good deeds or making good decisions. And it often comes from a place of insecurity. So when we feel bad about who we are—when we compare ourselves to others and decide we have the short end of the stick—we make things worse by trying to prove our worth through bragging.

But friend, God sees you even when others don't. He sees your effort. He knows your heart. He sees the amount of stress you carry because you desperately want to be noticed. And when you take your wounded heart to God, you'll experience freedom from the striving that's been driving you to self-promote. It will be enough to know the Lord fully understands all the wonderful and awesome ways about you.

## *Pray*:

*God, keep me from feeling the need to compensate for any jealousy I may be feeling by self-promoting. Speak value into my spirit so I know I am loved. Remind me I am seen and known. And let me find comfort knowing You see all the good things about me, so I don't have to boast to anyone to feel better. In Jesus' name I pray. Amen.*

# THE GOD OF ORDER

—————— Read 1 Corinthians 14:1–33 ——————

*Key Verse:*
*You see, the prophetic spirits are under*
*the control of the prophets because God*
*is the author of order, not confusion. This*
*is how it is in all gatherings of the saints.*
1 CORINTHIANS 14:32–33 VOICE

## Understand:

- Where does your life feel chaotic right now?

- Do you trust God to bring clarity? Have you asked Him for wisdom and discernment to better understand confusing situations?

## *Apply:*

Whenever there is chaos and stress, remember that situation isn't from God. He doesn't orchestrate confusion or anxiety. Yes, there may be mystery surrounding Him and things we may not understand. Remember our ways aren't His ways, and His thoughts aren't ours. But God is the Author of order. And He doesn't create situations to complicate your life. He isn't trying to muddy the waters.

Are you confused about the next right step to take in your career? Are you puzzled by the conversation with your friend and not sure where to go from here? Has the state of your finances bamboozled you? Are the lines of communication within your marriage blurred? Are you baffled by your child's response to your request? These are times to ask God for clarity. Ask Him to make straight the crooked path. Pray for discernment to see right from wrong and how to proceed. He'll bring order from chaos every time.

## *Pray:*

*God, sometimes I get lost in the chaos of my situation and want to give up. It's often hard to see through the fog and know the best next step to take. Details just confuse me, and I shut down. Bring clarity and truth to my heart so I can make sense of the current chaos I'm battling. I trust You and know You have my best in mind. I know You will make a way. In Jesus' name I pray. Amen.*

# THE VOICE OF GOD

—————— Read Psalm 29:1–11 ——————

## Key Verse:

*The voice of the LORD makes the lightning flash. His voice makes the desert shake; he shakes the desert of Kadesh. The LORD's voice shakes the oaks and strips the leaves from the trees while everyone in his Temple shouts, "Glory to God!" The LORD rules over the deep waters; he rules as king forever. The LORD gives strength to his people and blesses them with peace.*

PSALM 29:7–11 GNT

## Understand:

- Think about all the ways God has spoken to His children. How does He speak to you directly?

- Tell God where you need to hear from Him today.

## Apply:

Scripture talks about how powerful the voice of God can be. It can affect the weather. It can make land move at will. His voice is able to shake trees so violently that the leaves fall to the ground. With words, God can command the waters to obey His wishes. The Lord even spoke the heavens and earth into existence. Just His voice has the ability to break every law of nature that constrains mankind.

Sometimes we just need to hear God's voice to feel better about our situation. In those stressful moments when we're full of worry and fear, our humanity cries out for His divinity. We are desperate for the Holy Spirit's nudge to show us what to do next. We need God to speak to us through His Word or a song or a powerful sermon. There are times where His voice is the most important (and only) thing we need to get us to the other side of the struggle we are facing. In those times, ask for ears to hear Him and eyes to see it when He moves.

## Pray:

*God, I am looking and listening for You to speak into my situation. I am desperate to hear Your voice. In Jesus' name I pray. Amen.*

# THE PRIORITY OF PEACE

—————— Read Romans 14:1–23 ——————

## Key Verse:

*So then, make it your top priority to live a life of peace with harmony in your relationships, eagerly seeking to strengthen and encourage one another.*
ROMANS 14:19 TPT

## Understand:

- What are the things you strive for in life that keep you stressed out and stirred up? What would have to change so you could have peace?

- What are some practical ways you could focus on bringing peace into your relationships?

*Apply*:

What is your top priority? Are you striving to be popular? Do you want to make a name for yourself? Maybe you want to be organized and keep everyone on task. Are you trying to climb the corporate ladder? Are you more worried about being right than being kind? Do you want to look like the perfect family on social media? Are you rigid to a fault about your health routine? Are you chasing the proverbial fountain of youth? Take a moment and ask yourself if these may be contributors to the stress you've been struggling with.

God has something important that He wants to be your focus because He understands the value it adds to living. The priority the Lord has for you is a life of peace. And His hope and desire are that it infiltrates every part of your existence. From your relationships to your work to how you feel about yourself, God wants harmony to be present in your days and nights. Embrace it.

*Pray*:

*God, peace seems to elude me these days. I want it. I know You want it for me. But I end up focusing on excelling or winning or getting ahead, and I forget the value peace brings into everything. Help me grab hold of Your peace and let it reign in my life. Help me see how important it is for living and loving well. In Jesus' name I pray. Amen.*

# THE GOD WHO RESCUES

Read Isaiah 12:1–6

## Key Verse:

*See, God has come to rescue me; I will trust in Him and not be afraid, for the Eternal, indeed, the Eternal is my strength and my song. My very own God has rescued me.*
ISAIAH 12:2 VOICE

## Understand:

- Can you remember a time when God rescued you or someone you cared about? Replay that moment and recognize His faithfulness in it.

- In the past, how have you tried to rescue yourself? How did it turn out? What lessons did you learn?

## Apply:

There are so many situations where we feel we need rescuing. It could be feeling overwhelmed by the loss of someone we loved, and we can't seem to move on. It could be a difficult parent-child relationship where we feel as if we're losing ground. It could be a situation where we said yes but realize we need to walk away and are stressed at the thought of it. Or maybe it's a negative thought pattern that is burying us in shame, and freedom from it feels impossible. Maybe it's something entirely different. But regardless, every one of us will need saving, and God is ready and willing to do it.

Take a moment to tell the Lord where you're needing His help. Let God know where you're feeling stuck and unable to move forward. Share your fears and insecurities, asking for strength. And from this day forward, decide God will be the first One you call when you need rescuing. There's simply no substitute.

## Pray:

*God, I confess I've often considered myself the savior I needed most. I've looked to the world for remedies too. But nothing comes close to the magnificence of Your hand in my messy situations. Help me stay in a place of surrender to You so I can experience Your awesome power. In Jesus' name I pray. Amen.*

# ASK GOD TO REPAIR

—————— **Read 2 Corinthians 13:1–14** ——————

## Key Verse:

*Finally, beloved friends, be cheerful! Repair whatever*
*is broken among you, as your hearts are being knit*
*together in perfect unity. Live continually in peace, and*
*God, the source of love and peace, will mingle with you.*
2 CORINTHIANS 13:11 TPT

## Understand:

- Compare the differences between broken relationships where God intervened and the ones where
  you tried to fix them yourself. What stood out the
  most—good or bad?

- Identify ways you can live continually in peace in a
  world so full of heartbreak and stress.

## Apply:

An important part of any relationship is being willing to repair it when it breaks. And it will break, repeatedly. Any time you take two imperfect people living in an imperfect world trying to thrive in an imperfect union, there will be trouble. But when you think about it, it's in those hard seasons where we grow. Without them, there's no incentive to work on the rough edges and compromise. And when we bathe our relationships in prayer and ask the Lord to intervene, He will build them back into something beautiful.

Remember that God is the Source of all love and peace. Scripture clearly points to Him as the One we can access them through. So stop trying to fix it all yourself. Don't place all the burden and stress on your shoulders. Instead, be steadfast in going to God for help as you allow Him to knit your hearts together as one.

## Pray:

*God, relationships are so tricky and messy. That doesn't mean they aren't worth the effort; it's just what I've found to be the truth. And while I often want to cut my losses and walk away, I know it's important to repair what's broken. Please help me navigate these choppy waters. Be big in my situation and replace my stress with Your peace. In Jesus' name I pray. Amen.*

# HIS LOVE WON'T LEAVE YOU

—————— Read Isaiah 54:1–17 ——————

## *Key Verse:*

*"For even if the mountains walk away and the hills
fall to pieces, my love won't walk away from you, my
covenant commitment of peace won't fall apart."*
*The GOD who has compassion on you says so.*
ISAIAH 54:10 MSG

## *Understand:*

- What have you done that's made you think God
  would walk away? What is the truth?

- Ask God to tell you what He thinks about you.
  Spend time listening. Write them down.

## *Apply*:

Even if you mess up in marriage and it ends in divorce. Even if you scream at your kids and say horrible things. Even if you blow your budget so badly that it leads to bankruptcy. Even if you fall into a season where you give in to your fleshly desires more often than not. Even if you betray your best friend and she walks away. Even if your moral compass has been tossed aside. There is nothing that will take God's love away.

When we follow life down the wrong path, we often end up stressed out and worried that we've gone too far. We're concerned we may have pushed God too far away. And so rather than embrace the truth of His love and turn back toward Him, we run in shame. But friend, the reality is that it's never too late and you've not disappointed your way out of His love. Why not talk to God about it right now?

## *Pray*:

*God, I stress out sometimes thinking I've pushed too far or messed up too badly. What a relief to discover Your love won't walk away from me. I have lived in fear for so long, worried about being abandoned by You, but I now know it's impossible. Thank You for loving me despite my bad behavior. Help me live in ways that glorify You! In Jesus' name I pray. Amen.*

# THE IGNORANCE OF TURNING AWAY FROM GOD

———— Read Psalm 85:1–13 ————

## Key Verse:

*Now I'll listen carefully for your voice and wait to hear whatever you say. Let me hear your promise of peace—the message every one of your godly lovers longs to hear. Don't let us in our ignorance turn back from following you.*

PSALM 85:8 TPT

## Understand:

- How do you best hear God's voice? What message(s) do you long to hear from Him?

- Think about how you've handled stressful situations in the past. Has God played a key role? Have you trusted Him to help? What needs to change moving forward?

## Apply:

Turning away from God guarantees a rise in anxiety because we are literally walking away from our powerful source of peace. And while we may think we've got things under control, we don't. At least not for long. Keep in mind that we are severely limited by humanity. Even with our best intentions, we won't be able to replicate the peace God brings. Without it, we're left with second-rate substitutes and first-rate stress.

But what if we followed the psalmist's example and quieted ourselves to listen for God's voice? In those moments full of fear or insecurity, what if we waited expectantly for His words to calm our anxious heart? What if we recognized His direction would be the right direction to lead us out of chaos and into peace? Friend, the Lord has the perfect message to bring hope and comfort to your stressful situation. Keep your eyes and ears trained on Him.

## Pray:

*God, I confess the times I've turned away from You when You were exactly what I needed. Too often I've tried to fix things in my own way. Moving forward, I'm committed to listening for Your voice to guide me through those hard moments life brings. I want You to point me in the right direction. I want to follow You to the other side of the stress. In Jesus' name I pray. Amen.*

# KEEP THEM BLOOMING

———— Read Jude 1:1–25 ————

## Key Verse:

*Jude, a slave of Jesus the Anointed and a brother of James, to you, the ones whom God our Father loves and has called and whom Jesus, the Anointed One, has kept. Kindness, peace, love—may they never stop blooming in you and from you.*

JUDE 1:1–2 VOICE

## Understand:

- Besides kindness, peace, and love, what other things do you want the Lord to grow in you?

- What are some ways you can help the blooming process?

## Apply:

If you want to live a less stressed life, try focusing on kindness, peace, and love instead of everything that feels overwhelming. Maybe your test results came back from the doctor with concern. Maybe your child is struggling to make friends at the new school. Maybe your job description is changing, and you're worried. Maybe some old wounds have been triggered, and those messy, familiar feelings have come flooding back in. The easy thing to do is sit in the stress and pain. But choose to bloom.

Put a priority on showing kindness or loving others well. Find ways to be kind to a stranger. Take a meal to someone who needs help. Mow your neighbor's lawn or shovel their driveway. Volunteer your time at the shelter. Try to focus on peace by spending time with God through reading His Word, soaking in worship music, and praying. Let these things bloom in you so your sole focus isn't the negatives and stressors. Ask God to grow kindness, peace, and love so your heart will be on the right things.

## Pray:

*God, I love that a way to overcome stress is to change my focus. I can either sit selfishly in my mess or I can become more focused on others. I can wallow or I can serve. Open my eyes to see how I can show kindness and love to those around me and experience peace because of it. In Jesus' name I pray. Amen.*

# WHEN YOUR PATIENCE HAS WORN THIN

———————— Read Ephesians 4:1–16 ————————

## Key Verse:

*With tender humility and quiet patience, always demonstrate gentleness and generous love toward one another, especially toward those who may try your patience. Be faithful to guard the sweet harmony of the Holy Spirit among you in the bonds of peace, being one body and one spirit, as you were all called into the same glorious hope of divine destiny.*

EPHESIANS 4:2–4 TPT

## Understand:

- Would you consider yourself to have tender humility and quiet patience? Do you demonstrate gentleness and generous love toward those who try your patience? How could these be a reality for you?

- What's the difference between peace from the Holy Spirit and peace offered by the world?

*Apply:*

Today's verse is asking a lot, amen? Think about those times when your patience has worn thin because some-one is driving you nuts. You're about to explode in frustration. And you don't want to walk out peace because all you feel is anxiety. So when we're asked to have tender humility and quiet patience, it feels almost impossible. Suggesting we demonstrate gentleness and generosity toward the very ones who are driving us nuts seems ridiculous. But when we find the strength and will to make it happen, something beautiful comes about.

The Holy Spirit in us will help us make this a reality. We can't do this on our own. He'll help us guard the kind of harmony He wants us to share with one another. In Christ, we're on the same team. We may feel frus-tration from time to time, but to feel splintered is the Enemy's lie. Ask God for His unifying Spirit to create peace in your relationships.

*Pray:*

*God, alone I do not have what it takes to be humble, patient, gentle, or generous. Please replace my stress with Your peace from the Spirit so I can love and live well. In Jesus' name I pray. Amen.*

# THE DESIRE TO RELAX

--------- Read Isaiah 32:1–20 ---------

*Key Verse:*

*Then righteousness will yield peace, and the quiet and confidence that attend righteousness will be present forever. My people's homes and hometowns will be filled with peace; they'll relax, safe and secure.*
ISAIAH 32:17–18 VOICE

*Understand:*

- Think about how quiet and confidence, peace's companions, would change your life. Journal about it.

- What words in today's scripture stand out the most to you and why?

*Apply:*

If we were to be honest, we'd all admit a desperate desire to be able to relax rather than be stressed out and stirred up. Be it a crazy calendar, a wayward child, a financial breakdown, a loss of security, a broken marriage, or the grief that comes from loss, it's hard for us to find the space to rest. We struggle to feel safe and secure because we ricochet off one problem to the next. So how can we find peace?

Scripture says that when we live right with God, being deliberate to follow His ways, peace will find us. And its constant companions—quiet and confidence—will be with us too. So how do you live righteously? Start reading the Bible with intention, writing down passages or commands that stand out to you. Ask the Lord to highlight what He has for you in His Word so you don't miss it. And look at those around you who love God, watch how they live, and talk to them about their choices and decisions.

*Pray:*

*God, I love the idea of finding ways to relax. I want to feel safe and secure. And I now understand it's connected to living a righteous life, one pleasing to You. Help me be intentional with my time and treasure. Help me live focused on You. Grow my faith so it can keep me on the right path. In Jesus' name I pray. Amen.*

# MAY THE LORD

──────── Read Numbers 6:1–27 ────────

## Key Verse:

*"May the Lord bless and protect you; may
the Lord's face radiate with joy because of
you; may he be gracious to you, show you
his favor, and give you his peace."*

NUMBERS 6:24–26 TLB

## Understand:

- What part of today's scripture impacts you the
  most? Why?

- Who in your life could benefit from this passage?
  Who needs hope that things can get better? Make
  a plan to connect with them and share this powerful Word.

## *Apply:*

We've talked a lot about ways we can live a less stressed life, but how can we help others find peace through the chaos too? One of the most powerful verses offered in God's Word is today's reading. Let it be a gift you give to those around you when their lives feel out of control and riddled by anxiety. This passage is a hope backed by a promise, and it may be the cure for being weighed down by worry.

It's a hope for God's blessing. It's a desire for protection against the Enemy's plans. It's a powerful visual of His delight because of you. It's an expectation of God's generosity and favor in action that results in an overwhelming sense of His peace. This combination is potent, and it's available to everyone. So when you or someone you care about is drowning in stress and anxiety, let these verses be the net that catches and delivers you from the tumultuous waters of despair.

## *Pray:*

*God, thank You for verses like today's that remind us there is hope. Sometimes I'm so overwhelmed I forget, and sometimes I watch those I care for forget too. Bless us. Protect us. Let Your face radiate because of us. And Lord, be gracious, show favor, and bless Your children with peace. In Jesus' name I pray. Amen.*

# HOLY AND WHOLE

―――――― **Read 1 Thessalonians 5:1–28** ――――――

## Key Verse:

*May God himself, the God who makes everything holy and whole, make you holy and whole, put you together—spirit, soul, and body—and keep you fit for the coming of our Master, Jesus Christ. The One who called you is completely dependable. If he said it, he'll do it!*
1 THESSALONIANS 5:23-24 MSG

## Understand:

- In your opinion, what does it look like to be holy and whole?

- Do you believe God is completely dependable? What drives that opinion? Is it accurate?

## *Apply:*

Only God can make everything holy and whole. He's the One who can put you together and keep you that way regardless of the hard seasons you're facing. He will outfit you with tools to deal with stress and fear. When you rely on Him, you can rest knowing things will be okay in the end. You can trust God to be there because He is completely dependable.

The problem is that so often we carry the burden ourselves. We decide it's up to us to be holy and so we work toward it, eventually falling short. We lean on our own knowledge to make us whole but soon realize we aren't God. And the stress comes from trying to piece ourselves together when we don't have the skill set to do it. Friend, lean on the Lord. He makes everything holy and whole. And that includes you.

## *Pray:*

*God, why do I continue to try to be You? It's never gone well, but for some reason I keep trying to fix and control things in my life. Forgive me for stepping into Your place. Help me keep the right perspective so I know where I end and You begin. And let my surrender keep stress at bay so I can live in peace. In Jesus' name I pray. Amen.*

# GIVE IN TO GOD

———— Read Job 22:1–30 ————

## Key Verse:

*"Give in to God, come to terms with him and everything will turn out just fine. Let him tell you what to do; take his words to heart. Come back to God Almighty and he'll rebuild your life."*

JOB 22:21–23 MSG

## Understand:

- What emotions come with the idea of you giving in to God? Are they good emotions or bad? Explore why.

- Ask God to tell you what to do regarding the stressful situations you're facing. Spend time with Him in prayer and let Him give you much-needed direction.

## Apply:

We can be so stubborn, can't we? We bite onto an idea or concept, sinking our teeth deep and never wanting to let go. It's human nature to think we know best—to think our way is the right way—but our thinking never trumps God's. Never. So when we decide to push Him aside and stand in our own understanding, we'll find ourselves in big trouble.

Friend, why not let God lead? If the idea is to live a less stressed life, why not let Him tell you what to do next? He is the One who created the world and everything in it, right? He is perfect in every way, yes? Doesn't He know you better than you know yourself? And isn't He the One who determined your future? Right now, God is inviting you to trust Him with everything. He sees the stress. He understands the anxiety. And He has the exact answer to help you rebuild your life.

## Pray:

*God, I'm at a loss with how to move forward. Would You open my eyes to the path You have determined for me? Would You give me the ears to hear Your voice guide me? Today, I am surrendering my ideas and plans, and I'm waiting for You to reveal Yours instead. In Jesus' name I pray. Amen.*

# EYEING THE HEALTHY SOUL

---
### Read Psalm 37:1–40
---

## *Key Verse:*

*Keep your eye on the healthy soul, scrutinize
the straight life; There's a future in strenuous
wholeness. But the willful will soon be discarded;
insolent souls are on a dead-end street.*
PSALM 37:37–38 MSG

## *Understand:*

- What are some practical ways you can focus on
  having a healthy soul?

- What brings pollution into your life? How does
  pursuing strenuous wholeness combat it?

## Apply:

Sometimes in our frustration, we give in to stress and anxiety and accept them as the way things will always be. We invite them in, like we would a good friend. We make room in our day. And we learn to coexist as they eventually run the show. These two are deadly, though, and they'll take everything from you, leaving you feeling empty and hopeless. They're reckless with your heart and will bankrupt it in the end.

This is the exact reason why it's vital to keep our eyes on God, asking for His help as we focus on keeping our soul healthy. It's when we don't that it becomes polluted by outside sources. Yes, it's possible to be in a stressful situation and have peace. With God, we can rise above any fear and anxiousness. Make time to dig in to what godly living looks like and walk it out in your own life. When you are actively seeking wholeness, you will find it. Ask Him for perseverance and faith.

## Pray:

*God, help me focus on You so my soul isn't polluted by stress and fear. I know those keep me from experiencing joy and peace. They stop me from living with passion. And I don't want anything to disconnect me from the victory I have when I keep my eyes on You. In Jesus' name I pray. Amen.*

# A HOLY PURSUIT

—— **Read 2 Timothy 2:1–26** ——

### *Key Verse:*

*Run as fast as you can from all the ambitions and lusts of youth; and chase after all that is pure. Whatever builds up your faith and deepens your love must become your holy pursuit. And live in peace with all those who worship our Lord Jesus with pure hearts.*

2 TIMOTHY 2:22 TPT

### *Understand:*

- What are the ambitions and lusts of youth that still trip you up? How do they keep you from pursuing what is pure?

- Think about the things that build faith and deepen your love. What do they have in common?

## Apply:

Life is all about choices. We can choose to live stressed out or to live in peace. We can be full of anger or full of love. We can be selfish with our time and treasure or we can give and serve others. Our days can be marked with worry or we can activate faith instead. It's all a choice and it's up to you. But the direction you take makes a difference.

God's Word reminds us that if we're to chase after anything, it's to be what is pure. This means we choose to pursue a godly life with passion and purpose rather than falling into our old sinful ways. Is it time to let those old patterns and thoughts pass away and embrace the kind of living that glorifies the Lord? Let your holy pursuit be to build your faith and deepen your love. This guarantees peace over stress every day.

## Pray:

*God, help me willingly let go of the things from my past that keep me tangled in sin. I want to have a holy pursuit that strengthens my faith in You and encourages me to love others with gusto. Bless me with peace over stress so I can bloom as I grow in relationship with You! In Jesus' name I pray. Amen.*

# SLEEP WITHOUT WORRY

—————— Read Leviticus 26:1–45 ——————

## *Key Verse:*

*I will see to it that you have peace in your land. You
will be able to go to bed at night without a worry on
your mind. I will take away the dangerous animals that
roam your land, and no armies will invade your land.*
LEVITICUS 26:6 VOICE

## *Understand:*

- How often do stress and fear affect your sleep?
  What does it look like when it happens?

- In your life, have you found a way that allows peace
  and worry to coexist? What is the Holy Spirit saying
  to you about it right now?

## *Apply:*

Worrying about things is hard enough during the day, but so often it follows us to bed at night and keeps us awake. It's in those times when we've slowed down that our minds get busiest. When there aren't the usual distractions of family, work, chores, and appointments, idle time eats us up. This is when stress stirs us up and anxiety works overtime. Without a doubt, the dark of the night can be the toughest time for peace.

But God's peace is available twenty-four hours a day. It doesn't lose effectiveness after you turn off the lights. So when you crawl into bed, ask the Lord to cover your night with it. Every time your eyes pop open and your heart starts thumping faster, pray. Cry out for God to be with you. Ask for His comfort and calm. Tell Him what's stressing you out and ask for sweet dreams instead.

## *Pray:*

*God, nights are hard for me because the idle time stirs up my fears and worries. I finally slow down, but my mind doesn't. Help me go to bed at night worry-free so I can get the sleep I desperately need. Take the stress away so I can slumber in peace. In Jesus' name I pray. Amen.*

# YOU ARE SALT

---
Read Mark 9:1–50
---

## Key Verse:

*"Everyone will pass through the fire and every sacrifice will be seasoned with salt. Salt is excellent for seasoning. But if salt becomes tasteless, how can its flavor ever be restored? Your lives, like salt, are to season and preserve. So don't lose your flavor, and preserve the peace in your union with one another."*

MARK 9:49–50 TPT

## Understand:

- What kind of seasoning are you bringing into the world these days? Are you stressed and scared or full of faith? What needs to change?

- Spend time in prayer, asking God where He wants you to spice things up for Jesus in your sphere of influence. Ask Him for open doors.

## *Apply:*

If you're to be a seasoning for the world, imagine how being stressed out would render you tasteless. Your effectiveness would be bland. And rather than being a potent part of sharing God's Word with others, you'd be self-absorbed and ineffective. The reality is that few things cause us to lose our flavor more than being weighed down by worry and anxiety. Why? Because being hyperfocused on our own situation shuts down our faith. We stop looking at God and depending on Him to help. And it shows.

Friend, you have a job to do. Being a woman of faith is a beautiful call to point others to God through your words and actions, so it's important to do what it takes to keep your flavor alive. Spend time in the Word and pray every time your heart is prompted. Look for the Lord throughout your day, acknowledging His hand in your circumstances. Live in His peace and joy, and let it be contagious. And never forget you are salt.

## *Pray:*

*God, I want my faith to flavor the world for You. Help me see people and places where I can share Your goodness in my life as an encouragement. I love You so much! In Jesus' name I pray. Amen.*

# ABOUT THE AUTHOR

**Carey Scott** is an author, speaker, and certified Biblical Life Coach who's honest about her walk with the Lord—stumbles, fumbles, and all. With authenticity and humor, she challenges women to be real, not perfect, and reminds them to trust God as their Source above all else. Carey lives in Colorado with her two kids who give her plenty of material for writing and speaking. She's surrounded by a wonderful family and group of friends who keep her motivated, real, and humble. You can find her at CareyScott.org.